‘What will our nation look like in 2040? That is the central question posed by Tim Watts and Clare O’Neil in *Two Futures: Australia at a Critical Moment*, a must-read publication from two talented new federal members of parliament more concerned about a better and fairer future for Australia than the current valueless debates. There are two future scenarios for Australia. Clare and Tim would have us take the high road, while not ignoring the “black swan” possibilities. More strength to them. We need more of this future thinking.’

STEVE BRACKS,
former Premier of Victoria

‘An insightful contribution to the policy debate about the future of our country. The authors are to be congratulated for taking a longer-term view, and reflecting the importance of taking a purposeful stance in policy-making: one which provides a frame of reference for the longer term, in the face of the exigencies of the short term.’

CATHERINE LIVINGSTONE,
President, Business Council of Australia

‘In *Two Futures* Clare O’Neil and Tim Watts have tried to set out their thoughts about the big issues that we will all have to deal with in the next twenty-five years…They seek to understand how our world works now or, more importantly, why it doesn’t work, with fresh eyes. Most importantly and refreshingly, they are asserting the need for individual politicians to participate in the policy debate, think about the future, be brave and take a point of view, and read and write about ideas.’

LAURA TINGLE,
Political Editor, *Australian Financial Review*

CLARE O'NEIL is the federal Labor member for the seat of Hotham, in Melbourne's southeast. She was Australia's youngest-ever female mayor and has been a management consultant with McKinsey & Company. She studied public policy as a Fulbright Scholar at the Harvard Kennedy School.

clareoneil.com facebook.com/ClareforHotham @Clare_ONeil_MP

TIM WATTS is the federal Labor member for the seat of Gellibrand, in Melbourne's west. Prior to entering parliament he was a senior manager at Telstra. He has been a lawyer at Mallesons Stephen Jaques and studied at the London School of Economics.

timwatts.net.au facebook.com/timwattsmp @TimWattsMP

TWO FUTURES

AUSTRALIA AT A CRITICAL MOMENT

CLARE O'NEIL
& TIM WATTS

TEXT PUBLISHING MELBOURNE AUSTRALIA

textpublishing.com.au

The Text Publishing Company
Swann House
22 William Street
Melbourne Victoria 3000
Australia

First published in 2015 by The Text Publishing Company

Cover and page design by Imogen Stubbs
Typeset in Granjon and Firme by J & M Typesetting

Printed in Australia by Griffin Press, an Accredited ISO AS/NZS 14001:2004 Environmental Management System printer.

National Library of Australia Cataloguing-in-Publication entry
ISBN: 9781925240214 (paperback)
ISBN: 9781922253026 (ebook)
Title: Two futures : Australia at a critical moment / by Clare O'Neil and Tim Watts.
Subjects: Legislators—Australia—Forecasting.
Legislators' writings, Australian.
Social prediction.
Australia—Politics and government—2013–
Dewey Number: 328.3310994

This book is printed on paper certified against the Forest Stewardship Council® Standards. Griffin Press holds FSC chain-of-custody certification SGS-COC-005088. FSC promotes environmentally responsible, socially beneficial and economically viable management of the world's forests.

Clare: To Brendan and Elvie,
who fill my life with love, joy and meaning.

Tim: To my wife, Joyce, thank you for your sacrifices and support.
To my children, Audrey and Aaron, these ideas are for you.

CONTENTS

FOREWORD
by Laura Tingle IX

INTRODUCTION
The Long View 3

CHAPTER 1
Democracy 11

CHAPTER 2
Inequality 43

CHAPTER 3
Technology 73

CHAPTER 4
Climate 107

CHAPTER 5
Growth 133

CHAPTER 6
The World 173

CONCLUSION
Two Futures 207

ACKNOWLEDGMENTS 219

FURTHER READING 221

Foreword
by Laura Tingle

BEN CHIFLEY USED to drive himself from Bathurst to Canberra. John Curtin would catch the train from Perth. When Robert Menzies went to London, he went by boat. These were hours, days and weeks in which our prime ministers—and their contemporaries—were not just out of the news cycle but out of contact.

It was only in the 1993 election, just over twenty years ago, that mobile phones became part of the way parties campaigned. The need for politicians to immediately respond to something happening on the other side of the country—the fact they knew about it at all—changed the way election campaigns ran. Suddenly everything was all joined up. The previous difficulties for political staff—and journalists—of finding a phone near where a politician was campaigning vanished. The scope for politicians to say something different to their colleagues, because they were in a different part of the country, shrank.

The acceleration of the news cycle, and the message discipline that has sprung up in response to the leaps and bounds of technology, haven't just transformed what is reported in the media about politics each day: they have robbed our politicians of time to think, and the space to formulate ideas that don't fit into a neat sound grab.

Earlier technological constraints meant politicians could 'disappear' for a few days back home—particularly in the middle of a crisis or political conflict—to consider what their position should be, and where the long-term national interest might lie, with some detachment. Not anymore.

Finding time to think outside the news cycle, indeed having the capacity to think outside the news cycle, is now the challenge for all politicians.

Technology itself makes the challenge of identifying the big, long-term issues all the more difficult. We have already seen how technological transformation has changed not just politics but our economy in recent decades. Trying to establish some benchmarks for what will affect our quality of life in 2040 amid such static is even more difficult.

In *Two Futures* Clare O'Neil and Tim Watts have tried to set out their thoughts about the big issues that we will all have to deal with in the next twenty-five years, in politics and in the country as a whole: issues that get depressingly little mention in the parliament or in the news cycle.

Growth, technology, climate, inequality, Australia and the world, and democracy are all in their sights. As they say themselves, they are not overly prescriptive or specific. How can you be about what will be happening in twenty-five years' time? But they seek to understand how our world works now or, more importantly, why it doesn't work, with fresh eyes.

Most importantly and refreshingly, they are asserting the need for individual politicians to participate in the policy debate, think about the future, be brave and take a point of view, and read and write about ideas.

Two Futures

INTRODUCTION

The Long View

IN 1967, THE American futurists Herman Kahn and Anthony J. Wiener published *The Year 2000*. They predicted that by the closing decades of the twentieth century we would have an overabundance of leisure time: as technology made people more efficient, the working week would reduce to thirty hours, with thirteen weeks of annual leave. The book generated volatile discussion about the inevitable decay of such an idle society.

Thirty-odd years later, the Y2K bug loomed. It was predicted that computers around the world would shut down on New Year's Eve 1999, causing widespread chaos. In 1943 the head of IBM predicted that the world would only ever need a handful of computers. In 2007 the International Monetary Fund predicted that global growth would be almost 4 per cent in 2009: an estimate that, after the worst global recession since the Second World War, turned out to be a few trillion dollars wide of the mark.

Predicting the future is hard—a fool's game. Yet voters quite rightly demand that their elected representatives take the long view. The lack of long-term thinking is a frequent criticism of politicians, inspiring endless op-eds, thousands of university essays and a handful of TED Talks. Why isn't there more emphasis in public life on the decades ahead?

One reason is that our political process is built for the short term. The contemporary news cycle, in which media outlets churn through significant stories in hours, hungry for new material, favours politics that is all spin, no substance. With multiple news cycles a day for a government or opposition to win, there is constant distraction.

Then there is the sheer pace of modern politics. Together, across our two electorates, we represent 283,000 people. We each manage five or six staff. We receive and send about one thousand emails a week. We speak or write frequently in parliament and on television, in newspapers and on social media. We attend hundreds of community events every year. And we are backbenchers without portfolio duties.

Back in the day (the older pollies tell us) most politicians weren't expected to help much around the home. But we both have young children, and significant family responsibilities.

It's not true that politicians care only about the short term. There are far more earnest True Believers in office, on both sides of politics, than cynical Hollow Men. It's just that long-term thinking—for which there is no deadline and little prospect of return on effort—often gets lost in the fray.

For us, though, the long term is where it's at. Changing society takes time. That's why we ran for parliament: to be a part of that change. It's the only thing that could possibly justify us spending at least twenty-two weeks a year away from our families.

We believe that good governments always have an eye on the future. And we believe that, as new members of parliament, part of our job is to articulate what that future might be, what it may mean for Australians and how we can make the best of it. We wrote this book as a way of bringing structure and discipline to thinking about what we, as politicians in the early part of the twenty-first century, ought to be preparing for. And to sketch out ideas for what we want to accomplish over our political careers: some big, some small.

Plenty of research tells us why humans are bad at thinking about the future. A whole subset of behavioural economics is dedicated to explaining it. We've tried to avoid four common errors here.

The first is that people rely too much on emotion and not enough on evidence. Our approach is based on facts and data. The goal is less Nostradamus, more Nate Silver.

Second, people try to be too specific about the future, ignoring broad trends in favour of detailed possibilities. That's why our book is called *Two Futures*. Instead of predicting exactly what challenges Australia will face, in our Conclusion we describe two bookends. We think that Australia's future lies somewhere between them.

Third, futurists often try to predict too far ahead. We've chosen to talk about issues that are affecting Australia now, even if they are unfolding slowly. They are obvious problems, but most are not receiving the attention they deserve. And we've picked a manageable timeframe of twenty-five years.

Last, we ignore Black Swans: small-probability events with vast ramifications. Most of the events that defined the twentieth century—the Depression, world wars, the Holocaust, the rise of communism, the disintegration of colonialism, AIDS, the invention of the internet—could not have been predicted decades before they occurred. We have to assume that massive unpredictable events will occur, which is why strong institutions and resilience are recurring themes in this book.

○

Our first chapter examines the health of our representative democracy. The future, whether we plan for it or not, will require us all to make difficult decisions. Yet, today, our democracy is in trouble: low levels of public trust, a parliament that hasn't changed with the times. Without a robust, functional democracy, we're in for a painful ride.

Our second chapter is about rising inequality. Without policy change, inequality in Australia is likely to be much worse by 2040. We dig into the forces driving inequality and explore some of the answers: early-childhood education, vocational education and training, the role of unions, a fairer distribution of capital, and genuine social and economic inclusion of Indigenous Australians. Unless we make significant structural changes in these areas, we risk a widening rift between the rhetoric of egalitarianism and the reality of life in Australia.

In our third chapter we explore the Digital Revolution, which is changing how humans and machines interact, and how we organise our economy, society and culture. Online communities and digital data offer new ways to tackle the problems faced by businesses, communities and governments. Public policy will shape how we manage the risks and opportunities presented by life in the digital age. At the moment, the settings are wrong.

Next, we tackle climate change. For years, Australia has been locked in a toxic debate about how to decrease pollution. Meanwhile, the rest of the world has moved on—talking about more ambitious targets and competing to capture the big upside to acting early on climate change. We're better placed than almost any other nation to reap the benefits of tackling global warming and to efficiently transform our economy to a lower-pollution one. But only if we act soon. Whatever we do now, though, some level of climate change to 2040 is now inevitable. Life in all corners of the country will be affected. We need to begin a national conversation about how we're going to adapt.

Our penultimate chapter is about economic growth. Australia has experienced twenty-four years of uninterrupted growth. But the drivers of our most recent wave of prosperity are under pressure. Whether we have a thriving economy in 2040 will depend on whether we diligently continue the reform process, get serious about engaging with Asia, make a huge improvement to the quality of our education system, better manage and protect our natural resources, and create world-class innovation policies. Another long period of sustainable growth is possible, but we won't get there by coasting.

In the final chapter we turn to our neighbours in the Indo-Pacific. Their growth creates new strategic challenges for Australia. The United States' dominance of our region is ending and in its place a multipolar order is emerging. In the nineteenth and twentieth centuries Australia was forced to deal with the tyranny of distance; in the twenty-first it will need to deal with the problems of proximity.

Clare led our work on inequality, climate change and growth. Tim led on democracy, technology and Australia's place in the world. Readers should consider us individually responsible for the chapters where we took the lead. But, broadly, in *Two Futures* we speak as one.

We think that the six major challenges we discuss will determine our quality of life in Australia in 2040, and we share a commitment to the agenda outlined to tackle those challenges.

o

What might our nation look like in 2040?

Will we continue our history of democratic innovation, modernising our political institutions to reflect changing expectations and technologies? Or will Australians become more alienated from their elected representatives, allowing ideologues and special interests to dominate debate?

Will Australia be a country where the achievement gap that we see in four-year-olds dissipates in the first years of school, giving all children an equal chance at going on to university? Or will inequality continue to increase, driving the politics of envy as wages further diverge, and more wealth is concentrated at the very top?

Will Australians be at the vanguard of the Digital Revolution, creating new ways of producing goods and services, and reshaping our government? Or will the majority of people be excluded from the benefits of this revolution, competing for jobs with robots and algorithms that drive down their wages and conditions?

Will Australia lead the world in the development of new energy technologies and embrace the possibilities created by the transition to a low-pollution economy? Or will we fail to adapt, leaving the worst-off in our society vulnerable in a degraded environment and a second-rate economy?

Will Australia make the investments required to become a high-wage, innovative economy, and to integrate tightly with a growing Asia? Or will we drift into the future, more dependent on low-skill services, mining and agriculture, while the great economic opportunities within our grasp pass us by?

Will Australia become a Southeast Asian power, trusted by the great powers for its expertise and influence? Or will the nation decline in international standing, its voice lost among the clamour of ever larger and more powerful neighbours?

By 2040 the trends that we explore in the following chapters will change Australia. In good ways, if we manage the transitions well; and in bad ways, if we do not. These are our two futures.

1 Democracy

THIS IS A book about ideas. But we're not interested in ideas as weightless electrical charges in the minds of our readers. We want to turn thoughts into action.

The institutions of our representative democracy—our parliament, political parties and media—are Australia's change machine. Together, they take ideas about how to improve our society and make them reality. They are designed to aggregate and mediate public opinion, build coalitions, rally public support and resolve conflicts. And they are designed to hold governments accountable for their actions.

Influential economists such as Douglass North, Daron Acemoglu and James Robinson argue that the quality of democratic institutions is the fundamental difference between those nations which experience prolonged social and economic growth, and those which stagnate and fail. This has been the story of Australia's economic success to date. In *Why Australia Prospered* the economic historian Ian McLean argues that the strength and responsiveness of our democratic institutions—particularly their responses to external shocks like economic depressions, international financial crises and environmental events—have been central to Australia's sustained economic growth from European arrival to today. When Donald Horne described Australia as the 'lucky country' he was referring to 'the luck of its historical origins', the inheritance of Britain's democratic institutions, rather than any innate characteristic of the land or its people.

After a fractious decade there are signs that Australia's democratic luck is starting to run out. The conflict-ridden and electorally costly reform experiences of recent Australian governments have prompted some observers to say that the machinery of change in our country has broken, and that substantial reforms are now all but impossible. As the journalist and author George Megalogenis pointed out in 2012, 'the last big reform that landed safely and survived a change of government [in Australia]...was the GST, and that is a long time ago.' Fifteen years, in fact. The National Disability Insurance Scheme (NDIS) may well qualify as another enduring reform, depending on the actions of the current government, but beyond this the pickings are slim. Given the scale of the challenges that Australia will face over the coming decades, we cannot afford another twenty years in which we are unable to deliver enduring reform. Without healthy democratic institutions, we won't be able to shape the kind of future that we want for Australia in 2040.

To understand whether something is broken in our machinery of change we need to understand what is required to successfully deliver reform in a contemporary democracy. The findings of the Organisation for Economic Co-operation and Development (OECD) Making Reform Happen project make it clear that individual leadership and good ideas, while important, are not sufficient to achieve enduring reform in the developed world. Successful reforms also require effective communication, over time, to secure a mandate from the public on both the need for change and the new policy approach.

No individual leader, no matter how popular, can do this without healthy democratic institutions that are responsive and legitimate. Leaders rely on institutions that allow the desires and concerns of the public to be heard and mediated by political representatives, and in turn for the judgments of these leaders credibly to be conveyed to the community.

Historically, various institutions have served this purpose in Australia. The parliament provided a forum for elected members to represent the interests of their constituents and was a clearing house for conflicts between interests. Mass-membership political parties allowed people with shared values to act collectively to build support in the community for policies based on these values and to elect people to represent them. An editorially independent media provided a shared forum within which competing perspectives could be tested and political figures could shape public opinion.

These institutions were far from perfect, but throughout the twentieth century they allowed the public to be heard, and political leaders to form a judgment and make a case for change to the community. Now, major changes in citizens' expectations and technological capabilities mean that the institutions which served us so well in the twentieth century, with little change, are ever less effective in the twenty-first century.

○

Institutions do not exist in a vacuum. They are a product of the prevailing cultural and social norms, technologies and infrastructures of their times. Institutions that work well in one context, in one time, will flounder in another. Knighthoods may have made sense as a way of keeping order in mediaeval England, but almost no one has any use for them as an institution in today's Australia.

In his influential book *The End of Power*, Moisés Naím, a former executive director of the World Bank and editor of *Foreign Affairs* magazine, suggests that citizens around the world have undergone a 'revolution of mentality' in recent times. He argues that the spread of education, combined with growing prosperity, has increased individual aspirations and, as a result, people's expectations of democratic institutions.

Similar trends have been observed here. In her 2012 *Quarterly Essay*, Laura Tingle, political editor of the *Australian Financial Review*, examines the nation's sometimes contradictory attitudes towards government. 'Great Expectations' identifies a sense of both entitlement and resentment, and Australians' mounting frustration at the failure of our democratic institutions to satisfy their wants.

It's a frustration that wouldn't have been felt fifty years ago. Today, the Australian electorate is far better and more widely educated. In the 1960s, fewer than one in ten Australians had completed high school to Year 12 and around one in a hundred held a university degree. By 2012, almost half the population had a Year 12 education and almost one-fifth had a university degree. At the same time there has been a collapse in ideological affiliation after the Cold War and an accompanying decline in class identification as the catalyst for collective political action. The electorate is more informed, more assertive and less willing placidly to accept the received wisdom of a major political party.

Australian citizens' growing sense of agency is also fuelled by their experiences as consumers. Businesses strive to tailor offerings to individual tastes wherever possible and consumers expect to be able to deal with companies on their own terms. Instead of forcing customers to wait in line or on the phone for service, traditionally slow-moving organisations like banks and telecommunications companies now provide customer service in a range of ways adapted to individual preferences: via social media, live chat and community crowd-sourcing. Gyms and sporting clubs offer membership options designed to attract and engage every possible stripe of potential member. The age of one-size-fits-all service from large organisations is over.

As we discuss in detail in the Technology chapter, the emergence of the internet and the ease with which citizens are able to find like-minded individuals for even the most obscure areas of interest has led to a proliferation of niche political groups that would not have been viable on a similar scale in the past. Organisations like Every Australian Counts, Ban Live Export, Lock the Gate and the Asylum Seeker Resource Centre are now able to use the internet to harness the latent political engagement of Australians divided by geography but united by a shared interest in a specific issue. It's become common for people to bypass traditional, broad-based institutions of political engagement like the major political parties and to engage with politics in a way that reflects their preferences, issue by issue.

Despite these changes in citizen expectations and technological capability, for the most part the institutions of our democracy have not evolved. And you don't need to have many conversations with Australians before someone tells you that our democracy has never been in worse shape. Indeed, the 2014 Australian Constitutional

Values Survey found that more than one in four Australians think that democracy does 'not work well at all' or does 'not [work] very well' (only around one in eight thought the same thing in 2008). According to the Lowy Institute Poll 2013, only 59 per cent of Australians believe that 'democracy is preferable to any other kind of government.' Depressingly, enthusiasm is even lower among young voters, with the same survey finding that just under half of Australians aged eighteen to twenty-nine prefer democracy to the alternatives offered. Most striking of all, the Scanlon Foundation's 2013 Social Cohesion Survey found that respondents' second-most-common answer to the open-ended question 'What is the most important problem facing Australia today?' was the 'quality of government and politicians'.

○

Some may argue that Australians have always been cynical about politicians, political parties and the press, and that this alone shouldn't be taken as evidence of a crisis in our democracy. So let's scratch beneath the surface of these findings. The World Bank's Worldwide Governance Indicators research project looks in depth at what matters to the health of democratic institutions, in an effort to help developing economies improve their governance. It's not an exact science, but some academics have built on this research to suggest that the health of democracies in developed countries can be assessed by looking at voters' confidence in the effectiveness of democracy, their trust that governments will deliver on stated aims, their engagement and participation in electoral politics, the strength of political parties, and an open media environment. An examination of these metrics paints a bleak picture of the state of Australia's democratic institutions.

Almost all the available research shows that Australians have less confidence in the efficacy of their democracy than ever before. The 2014 Australian National University – Social Research Centre poll found that just 6 per cent of Australians had 'a great deal' of confidence in federal parliament. The Australian Constitutional Values Survey 2014 found that the proportion of Australians who have a 'very good' or 'great deal' of trust in the federal government to carry out its responsibilities fell from 81.6 per cent in 2008 to 52.5 per cent in 2014. A survey undertaken by the Centre for Advancing Journalism in 2013 found that over 70 per cent of Australians had 'not much' or 'no' confidence in the federal government and that a majority believed the quality of political leadership was noticeably worse today than it had been in the past.

There have been similarly significant falls in people's trust that our political leaders and institutions are acting in the public interest. The Australian Election Survey records that, in 1969, over 50 per cent of Australian voters believed that politicians could be generally trusted. Today the figure has fallen to 34 per cent. Similarly, just over one in four respondents to the 2013 Scanlon Social Cohesion Survey indicated that 'the government in Canberra can be trusted to do the right thing for the Australian people' always or most of the time (down from close to one in two in 2009). Less than 40 per cent of respondents to this survey could muster even 'some trust' in federal parliament.

Unsurprisingly, Australians are also participating less in electoral politics. When asked, they claim to be highly engaged with electoral politics, but this professed interest has not translated into political action. According to the Australian Election Survey, 73 per cent of Australians claimed to have discussed politics with others before the 2013 federal election, while almost nine in ten people professed to doing the same before the 1993 election. Almost half of Australians sought to persuade others about how they should vote at the 1993 federal election, but just 14 per cent claimed to do so in 2013.

This disengagement extends to the voting process. In the 2013 federal election one in five people aged eighteen to twenty-five—around four hundred thousand Australians—failed to enrol to vote. In the election that followed one of the closest results in the nation's history, and subsequently a minority government, the equivalent of four federal electorates' worth of young voters disenfranchised themselves.

Those who are enrolled are ever less likely to vote. Almost one million enrolled voters failed to turn up at the ballot box in 2013. And more of those who do turn up are also tuning out. In 1977 the nation-wide informal rate for ballots cast in the House of Representatives was 2.5 per cent. By 2013 it had more than doubled, to 5.91 per cent: a loss of hundreds of thousands of votes. Our colleague Andrew Leigh has estimated that in recent elections around a tenth of Australian citizens did not participate, by failing to enrol, failing to vote or voting informally. Comparing this outcome with historical data, he argues that 'voter disengagement is higher than at any time since the 1920s.'

Worrying patterns of disengagement can also be seen in the institutional hinges between the parliament and the electorate: our political parties. As the political scientists Anika Gauja and William Cross have highlighted, membership of political parties in Australia has fallen by around three-quarters as a proportion of population since the 1960s. Membership of the Liberal Party seems to have peaked at around 156,000 in the 1940s, dropping to around 78,000 today. Membership of the Labor Party has been more tumultuous, falling from around 75,000 to around 45,000 after the split with the DLP in the 1950s, then moving back up to around 54,000 after recent party reforms. These declines are all the more significant given the relative growth in the Australian population over this time.

Australia's political parties are losing supporters as well as members. According to the Australian Electoral Survey, the number of Australians who claim to 'always vote for the same party' has collapsed from 72 per cent in 1967 to 46 per cent in 2013. Voters are not just switching their allegiances between the major political parties: they are abandoning them altogether. As late as the 1983 federal election, the major parties accounted for 92.8 per cent of the vote; at the last federal election this figure had fallen to 78.6 per cent. That's well over a million voters who have withdrawn their support for the major parties.

Like them or loathe them, major political parties are the brokers of Australian democracy. They mediate between the myriad conflicting voices in the electorate and the relatively small number of voices in the parliament. They give citizens access to political decision-making in a way that direct democracy or a pure parliamentary democracy never could, given the size of our population. Without them, collective action in our democracy, both in our parliament and in our community, would be unimaginably difficult.

As support for major political parties has declined, support for independents and minor parties has increased commensurately. The cross-benches of the upper houses of Australian parliaments have never been more crowded with minor-party politicians. We've also seen a similar increase in the support for independent candidates in our lower houses. From federation to 1990, only thirteen independent members were elected to the federal House of Representatives. Between 1990 and 2013 alone, there were eleven. The result is what the British Labour commentator Hopi Sen has called 'kaleidoscope politics', a parliamentary configuration that is fragmented, frequently changing and much more difficult for political leaders to manage.

A large and diverse cross-bench poses problems for governments seeking to negotiate the passage of their policy agenda. These negotiations can be particularly problematic when the minor party knows that its political existence depends on representing a narrow set of interests, and hence feels no compulsion to consider the broader public interest or public opinion when forming its positions.

A more troubling characteristic of this growth in minor-party support is the anti-politics nature of parties such as the Greens and the Palmer United Party. Minor parties sometimes campaign from a position of being either above or opposed to politics as usual. This can mean campaigning against the kind of compromise and negotiation that are essential elements of a functioning representative democracy. In this way, these minor parties both encourage and benefit from the alienation of the electorate from our democratic institutions.

All of these changes contribute to making political life for our leaders nasty, brutish and short. The declining strength of institutions has been accompanied by an increased focus on individuals, particularly leaders, as the source of power in our democracy. This has created unprecedented levels of political instability. Political commentators frequently condemn the leadership changes of the previous federal Labor government, but what the BBC journalist Nick Bryant has called a 'coup culture' can be seen in both major political parties. In one extraordinary period between 2005 and 2008, there were twenty changes of leadership across the federal, state and territory parliaments in the Coalition parties.

In today's politics, the revolving door spins ever faster. In the forty-five years between the end of the Second World War and

1990, just fourteen individuals led Australia's major political parties at the federal level. In the twenty-five years since 1990, there have been sixteen leaders of the two major parties and Australia has on average seen almost two leadership changes every parliamentary term. Between 1975 and 1984, there was an average of three and a half leadership changes per year across the federal, state and territory governments. Between 2004 and 2014, the number of changes had leapt to five and a half per year. As a result, the leader of a political party in 2013 could reasonably expect to hold the position for around four hundred days fewer than could a leader in the 1970s or 1980s.

Rapid turnover of leaders is not intrinsically negative. Like the directors of companies or other organisations, political leaders must be accountable to the system that elects them. There are some countries where leaders hold power for decades unchallenged, and this can reflect a failure of accountability. But, at the same time, the pace of turnover of political leadership has real costs for our democracy. In addition to yanking political parties in different directions at the behest of new leaders, there is the loss of institutional memory and experience. These days, former leaders will often quickly leave parliament. New generations of parliamentarians must learn the lessons of politics without the benefits of on-the-job mentoring.

○

The media is a critical part of Australian democracy, as an essential interface between the public and its elected representatives. Yet the decline in traditional advertising revenues, particularly classifieds revenues, and the emergence of social media have radically changed the sector. The new media environment that has emerged in the twenty-first century is more fragmented, frantic and fanatical than ever. Each of these developments exacerbates the negative trends within the other democratic institutions we rely on in our political system.

One of the strengths of the media environment in the twentieth century was that it was a shared space. Political leaders could walk through the Canberra press gallery, buttonholing the journalists and editors of major news outlets to argue the case for reform in depth and in detail before stories were disseminated to the electorate. At the end of the process, most Australians saw a broadly recognisable version of the same debate presented in their newspapers and on their television screens each night.

This is no longer the case. According to the Australian Election Survey, in 1969 more than six in ten Australians claimed to follow news about the federal election on television 'a good deal'; by 2013 that figure had more than halved, to just three in ten. In the same survey, 55 per cent of Australians claimed to follow the 1969 federal election in newspapers 'a good deal'; by 2013 that figure had collapsed to just 17 per cent. If you want to see how much things have changed, ask a member of Generation Y whether they have *ever* watched the six o'clock news.

More Australians are following politics online, particularly through social media, but the internet offers a different version of the public sphere. Instead of citizens being presented with a political debate taking place within common frames of reference, citizens can choose to access voices online that discuss only the debates, indeed only the facts, suiting their political predilections. A 2015 study in *Science* magazine confirmed this effect among politically engaged Facebook users, finding that the combination of individuals' preferences for news that reinforces their pre-existing political views and a

Facebook algorithm that gives users more of the kinds of content that they already like 'limit[s] exposure to cross-cutting content'.

Instead of needing to persuade a handful of journalists and editors of the merits of a particular reform, political leaders must persuade millions of online voices directly. Instead of a shared public sphere in which political legitimacy can be built through argument, we have a plethora of interest networks that rarely intersect and often serve to confirm citizens' existing views. While it is undoubtedly a good thing that more Australians now have a direct political voice, it's come at a cost.

For a time in the twentieth century, much of the print media was sensitive to its role in facilitating considered public debate. Before publication, sources were checked, claims were weighed, and alternative views sought and considered. Now, much of the public sphere has become frantic, prioritising the production of sensationalist ephemera over the boring ballast required to underpin genuine democratic deliberation.

Spending weeks reading and talking to experts about the increasing complexity of policy issues in a globalised and interconnected world is not rewarded in this environment. The return on investment for journalists' time is far higher on yarns about political process and tactics, outrage and opinion: it's cheaper content to produce and less likely to be demonstrably wrong. The media cycle is no longer a slow-moving wheel rolling public deliberation forward with the addition of new facts and argument; it is a stationary washing machine on perpetual spin cycle, going nowhere and producing little more than froth.

The inevitable consequence of this fragmented and frantic environment is an increase in fanaticism. Objectivity and independence were perhaps the most treasured and fiercely guarded journalistic values of the media in the twentieth century. For the majority of journalists today, these values are still pre-eminent. But the voices of objectivity and independence are being shouted down by the louder and more influential voices of polarised politics. In an environment in which fewer Australians are consuming political news of any kind, the remnant audience for this kind of journalism is diehard partisans. We've seen a proliferation of news publications and political television shows that make no pretence of broad appeal, and instead make a transparent play for niche groups of political partisans.

Public trust in the media is now extremely low. In fact, journalism is one of the few professions in Australia distrusted more than government (though it still has a slight edge over those perennially maligned car salespeople). One survey conducted in the last days of the Gillard government found that, while confidence in the government had plummeted, confidence in the media had fallen even further, with 73 per cent of the population having no or not very much confidence in the print press. The 2015 Roy Morgan survey of trust in professions found that only 18 per cent of Australians believe newspaper journalists or TV reporters have high standards of ethics and honesty. As the strength of our media crumbles, so too does an important external buttress to our declining electoral institutions.

○

If the health of Australia's democratic institutions has been the foundation of its economic success to date, we've got good reason to be concerned about our future. On current trends, without conscious action, these institutions will continue to lose legitimacy in the eyes of our citizens and become less responsive to their concerns. Over time, the capacity of government to respond to external shocks and other changes in circumstances will diminish, putting our future prosperity at risk. In order to tackle the challenges of the coming decades, Australia needs first to modernise its democratic institutions.

This is a daunting challenge. Our democracy is a complex system, the health of which depends on the interactions of a large number of actors and institutions, often with competing incentives. Systemic change is a slow process and can't be forced. Indeed, no one actor can fix the problems of a complex system alone. Enduring change relies on broad support from all parts of the system, and the time won't be right for many reforms just yet.

That said, the eminent English political scientist Philip Norton, who has studied the way change occurs in parliamentary institutions like our own, argues that the conditions for change eventually align within a system to present windows of opportunity for reform. But this in itself is not enough for change to occur. There needs to be some intellectual heavy lifting first. A broad consensus needs to emerge on the problems to be solved. Ideas then need to be debated and solutions devised, so that they are ready to be implemented when the opportunity arises. To this end, we want to present a number of suggestions to improve the responsiveness and legitimacy of our institutions—ideas that we think are worth debating and trialling in the coming years.

○

The late Rob Chalmers, a member of the parliamentary press gallery from the Chifley government to the Gillard government, recounted a tale that illustrates how much the relationship between voters and government has changed. When Ben Chifley was prime minister, the story goes, there was a direct telephone line to the prime minister's office. While this number was not published, it was only one digit removed from the number of a local butcher's shop. Inevitably, every now and then a Canberra resident would call to make their weekly order of chops and mistakenly get through to the prime minister. Unperturbed, Chifley would take the order and pass it on to the butcher on behalf of his oblivious caller.

The days when our political leaders could take meat orders on behalf of citizens are long gone. When Ben Chifley was prime minister, members of parliament represented electorates with an average of around forty thousand constituents. Today, they represent on average ninety to one hundred thousand constituents. The scale of the task of being responsive to the interests of the electorate has changed radically.

At the most basic level, we need to make Australia's democratic institutions more responsive to the ways in which citizens want to engage with them. In the twenty-first century, this means enabling online engagement. The internet isn't a perfect medium for political engagement. Far from it. Women, in particular, are currently exposed to extraordinary levels of abuse when engaging in political debate online. But every mode of democratic engagement in history has been flawed in some way. We shouldn't disregard the potential of the internet because of its imperfections; rather, we should seek to improve the space.

We need to build digital institutions in which public opinion can be aggregated in a sensible and representative way for consumption by members of parliament. Online communities are already vigorously engaging with many of our existing democratic institutions, as anyone who's followed the question time and Senate estimates hashtags on Twitter can attest. We just need to let them in, so that they can be a part of these institutions.

We propose two ideas for harnessing this latent online political engagement and improving the responsiveness of our democratic institutions: allowing issues-based organising within political parties and establishing a forum for citizens' business in our parliament.

○

Advocates of internal reform in the Labor Party have long seen the internet as a panacea for the problem of member disengagement. Despite this, Labor's efforts to engage its members in internal party processes online have not resulted in a revolution in member participation. While recently the party has had success in developing online communications and fundraising relationships with supporters, mechanisms designed to allow online participation in the party have been less successful. Most initiatives have either been tokenistic bolt-ons to the organisational processes of the party or have merely replicated online existing organisational structures. They have either been powerless or have offered nothing new beyond their form. To build a more responsive political organisation, we need to build institutions which enable supporters to help realise the political outcomes they are seeking in the way that they choose, while also retaining the ability for the party to resolve conflicts between competing interests and present a coherent agenda to the public.

We propose the creation of a new institution within the Labor Party: the Online Policy Action Caucus (OPAC). All party members could be given the right to establish OPACs that advocate on specific issues (for example, Labor for Ethical Live Cattle Exports or Labor for Equal Marriage), without organisational approval, if they are able to sign up at least fifty existing party members to each group. A special class of membership could then be created to allow members of the general public to join not the Labor Party proper but a specific OPAC, for a nominal fee. OPACs that achieve a predetermined organising goal, such as signing up five thousand members to their group, could have the right to move an amendment to the party platform at the relevant national or state conference. The amendment would then be voted on by elected delegates in the normal way.

Such a model would give Labor members and supporters a clear incentive for political organising: they'd be able to have their issue debated at a Labor Party conference, the highest forum for debate in the party. It would allow fellow travellers to determine the nature of their engagement with Labor, enabling them to pursue a specific cause within the party without having to make the full commitment to party membership. It would also enable people to choose the means by which they engage with the party and other members; if other single-issue campaigning groups are anything to go by, much of the organising activity of these groups would occur online.

This would open up the Labor Party to participation by people in the community who may never have considered joining a political party, creating a large target pool of prospective members. Members of OPACs would also be a campaigning asset for the party. It's easy to imagine OPACs being a source of volunteers or micro-donors for MPs who agree to champion their issues.

In effect, the party would give up some central control over its internal agenda in exchange for increased engagement with supporters who, while sympathetic to the Labor cause, are more passionate about a single issue than an overarching ideology. OPACs would inject new voices into the internal policy-development processes of the party and build a culture of debate into the party's structures. At the same time, the existing party membership framework would ensure that the Labor Party's election platform was cohesive and the voice of single-issue groups did not drown out that of the broader membership. All it would take to realise this greater engagement is a little bit of democratic innovation.

Parliament, too, should use online engagement to improve its responsiveness to the community. The way parliament currently chooses the issues it will discuss is determined by the government, the opposition and occasionally individual MPs. It's a natural outcome of an era where parliamentary speeches were delivered for those in the chamber rather than those watching from outside it. Thanks to the internet, there is now no obstacle to allowing members of the public to play a direct role in setting the agenda of parliament.

We propose that a proportion of every parliamentary sitting week be dedicated to citizens' business, in which Australian citizens directly propose topics for debate by their elected representatives. These topics would be selected by the online votes of their fellow citizens. The selection of questions via peer voting of this kind is a common way of aggregating sentiment on social-media sites like reddit, Yammer and Facebook, and could easily be adapted to fit our parliamentary institutions. The Finnish parliament already requires a parliamentary debate and the vote of all members of parliament on the substance of any motion that attracts more than fifty thousand online signatures.

A platform that enables Australians to vote online to determine the issues that their MPs debate would give parliamentarians direct feedback about the strength of community sentiment on particular issues, and give citizens concerned about those issues the satisfaction that their parliament was engaging with them. And allocating regular time for citizens' business would not only improve the responsiveness of the parliament. People would be encouraged to engage potential fellow travellers to support the issue they are proposing, broadening community engagement. Moreover, people who vote on these topics would have a vested interest in watching their elected representatives debate these issues. They could gain a greater appreciation for the kinds of broader trade-offs that members of parliament will confront when they are forming a position on the issue.

○

In a democratic system, the most powerful source of legitimacy is the popular consent of the governed. (As Dennis the Peasant in *Monty Python and the Holy Grail* reminds us, leaders require a mandate—the support of the masses, not the Lady of the Lake waving Excalibur.) At the most basic level, legitimacy requires that our democratic representatives are elected in a way that reflects the will of the people. But how decisions are made and power is exercised by properly elected representatives, and how this is *seen* to be done, also matters.

Given that most citizens will rarely engage with the parliament it's important that, when they do turn their attention to Capital Hill, they are not confronted with conventions or symbols that are irrelevant to their experience as Australians or, worse, actively exclude them. As the former long-time Clerk of the Senate Harry Evans has noted, parliamentary anachronisms, even purely symbolic ones, are 'far from harmless. They convey a strong impression [to the public] of parliament as an antiquated and decorative institution with no substantial function.' Many of the symbols of our democratic institutions were developed at a time when Australia's attitudes and demographics were radically different.

At present, parliamentary sitting days begin with the Speaker reading a prayer for the parliament and the Lord's Prayer. While such a practice may have been understandable in 1911, when 96 per cent of Australians identified as Christian in the first Census to ask this question, it is surely not today. In the pluralistic, multi-faith society that Australia has become, the parliamentary sponsorship of a single religion is unnecessarily exclusionary. For this reason, despite growing up in Christian families, neither of us attends the chamber during these prayers: symbolic acknowledgment that the ritual unnecessarily excludes large numbers of our constituents.

The 2011 Census revealed that 61 per cent of Australians identify as Christian; but more than one in five Australians, almost five million people, reported that they have 'no religion', a figure that has risen steadily since the 1970s. Australia's fastest-growing religion, according to the 2011 Census, is Hinduism; yet, if any of the quarter of a million Australian Hindus tuned in to hear the Indian prime minister Narendra Modi's historic address to parliament in 2014, they would have been forced to listen to Madam Speaker recite the Lord's Prayer before being able to hear him, or any of Australia's democratically elected representatives, speak. If any of the nearly half a million Islamic Australians attended parliament to hear the prime minister's recent assurance that anti-terrorism legislation was not directed towards their religion, they would have heard the same thing.

Why does the formal opening of our parliament in the first sitting after a federal election begin with an address from the Queen's representative? Historically, the monarch summoned the parliament to advise on the interests of the realm. Yet this has not been the constitutional reality in the United Kingdom for centuries, and it is irrelevant to Australia in the twenty-first century.

In our view, as part of the constitutional recognition of Indigenous Australians, we should remove the Crown from the opening of parliament and, in its place, bring the Welcome to Country—currently performed earlier in the day, elsewhere in the parliament—into the chamber. Placing Australia's Indigenous heritage at the centre of our representative democracy would be far more meaningful for most people than an anachronistic royal ceremony and would better acknowledge the First Australians as the real founders of our national legitimacy.

A number of parliamentarians have in the past raised concerns about anachronisms of this kind, yet attempts to update them have been repeatedly rejected. However, since the 2008 parliamentary Apology to Australia's Indigenous Peoples (a powerful symbol in its own right), each sitting day has started with an Acknowledgment of Country from the Speaker, recognising that the parliament meets on the lands of the Ngunnawal and Ngambri peoples, and paying respect to the elders, past and present, of all Australia's Indigenous peoples. This symbolic recognition is something that all Australians can watch with pride, and it demonstrates that change is possible. It's something that we can build on as we seek to improve the parliament's legitimacy in the eyes of the public it represents.

○

It's difficult not to be embarrassed by the state of question time every sitting day. While we're participants in the circus and just as responsible as anyone else, we can't be the only members who have looked up into the public galleries and wondered what the teachers escorting school trips to parliament tell their students about the behaviour of MPs when the spectacle has concluded. Parliamentary microphones pick up only a tiny fraction of the noise, as they are in close proximity to the speaker, so one day Tim ran a noise-meter application on his iPad in the chamber. He found that the noise on the floor of parliament sometimes exceeded 130 decibels while the prime minister was speaking, equivalent to the sound of a four-engine jet from a distance of thirty metres.

In many ways, question time has become ground zero of the contempt cycle that has encircled Australian politics. For most Australians, the quick grabs from question time on news reports are the only window they have into the work of the parliament. It affords a view of the parliament at its worst behaved and least productive. As the Hansard Society has written in the British context, 'Prime Minister's Questions in Westminster is a "cue" for the public's wider perceptions of parliament—it provides a lot of the raw material that feeds their negative assumptions about politicians.' The hard grind of parliamentary committees, Senate estimates and legislative debates is overwhelmed by the ugly clamour for a news grab in the brief hour that the chamber is full.

Whether or not behaviour in question time is any better or worse than it used to be, standards of behaviour outside the chamber have changed. The bullying, abuse and carry-on of federal parliament would not be tolerated in any other contemporary workplace. Polling undertaken for the Hansard Society about the British population's attitudes to the far-better-behaved Prime Minister's Questions found that nearly half of those surveyed believe MPs do not behave professionally, nearly half believe 'it's too noisy and aggressive' and two-thirds believe 'there's too much party-political point-scoring instead of answering the question.' You shudder to think what Australians make of our debased colonial version. Question time is alienating and self-indulgent. If we want to enhance the legitimacy of our political leaders, we can't ignore the corrosive effect of this spectacle on public opinion of our democratic institutions.

For some years now, prime ministers and ministers from both major parties have flagrantly ignored the substance of the questions put to them in favour of either repeating talking points about the government's achievements or launching personal attacks on members of the opposition. The answer to a question from the opposition differs little today from an answer to a Dorothy Dixer placed in advance with a government backbencher. The old saw that 'It's called question time, not answer time' has never been truer.

The opposition treats these answers with the contempt they deserve. But mostly it's for naught. As the sole objective of question time for both sides is to get the best grab, first through the political followers on Twitter and the online news outlets, then through afternoon radio and, finally, on the evening news, the structural advantages of the format mean that the prime minister will always have a greater opportunity to speak for longer and to look the most authoritative.

According to OzTAM ratings, fewer than one hundred thousand people watch the afternoon television broadcast of question time on any given day of the week. More than three-quarters of these viewers are aged fifty-plus, meaning they're statistically less likely to be swinging voters. Changing this would change MPs' behaviour. Moving question time to the evening, in prime time, and directing ABC News 24 to broadcast it, even if it's only once every parliamentary sitting, would improve the behaviour of participants. Even a modest increase in the number of people watching parliament is likely to trigger negative feedback from those who matter most to MPs: their constituents. Broadcasting question time in prime time would also take it out of the evening media cycle, reducing the pressure on participants to secure the all-powerful news grab.

In addition to moving question time to a time slot that enables more Australians to view it, the session's structure needs to be changed to make it watchable. To maximise the potential audience for question time, we need to learn the production lessons of sports coverage and reality television. We don't mean that MPs should be able to be voted off the island (although a few candidates instantly spring to mind), or that coverage should be dumbed down—just that parliament should be broadcast in a way that accommodates a broader audience. If we use commentators to explain sporting contests to viewers, we should do the same with parliament. The broadcast of the proceedings should include text and graphics on screen intelligently explaining what is occurring at any time and providing explanations of key terms. Tweets and other social-media contributions from the public and MPs about the proceedings should also be included on screen.

The length of time allocated to answers needs dramatically to be shortened to increase the pace of the proceedings. Dorothy Dixers should be axed, minimising the repetition and predictability of the format. Citizens should be allowed to pose questions online that could be selected through real-time peer voting and asked of the relevant minister by the Speaker.

These changes would put the government at a disadvantage, so to even things up we should also adopt the British system of rotating topics for question time and specify in advance a limited number of ministers who could be called upon to answer questions on any particular day. The days on which the prime minister could be asked questions would then be the obvious candidate to be broadcast in prime time.

Questioning different ministers on specific days means that the questions couldn't always directly come from, and then feed back into, that day's hottest media story—which could assist in slowing the media cycle. A rotation approach to question time would increase the chances that the parliamentary debate would focus on policy substance, rather than on passing trivia or personal attacks. It would also lessen the public impression the prime minister is single-handedly responsible for absolutely everything in government, and so reduce the leader-centrism of media coverage.

Another, more radical option is to adopt a more intimate format for these sessions, without the bear-baiting dynamic of the full chamber. Senate estimates hearings are generally conducted in more respectful tones than question time. A form of question time that involved fewer members in a smaller space would be a dramatic break with tradition, but it would also be much more likely to produce a productive dynamic in the room. It's difficult to be as combative and insulting to someone sitting five metres from you as it is to someone sitting twenty metres away.

○

We cannot fight the shift away from the consumption of mass-circulation newspapers and mass-audience television news, but there are small interventions that would help shape the splintered public sphere that is emerging in their place. First, we can improve the financial viability of high-quality outlets. Giving news organisations that sign on to the Press Council's standards of practice and agree to binding adjudications tax deductibility under Australian taxation laws could be one useful step. Such a move may assist the long-term viability of smaller, high-quality media outlets. It should be recognised that the measure would indirectly undermine the independence of media outlets with respect to the government, to a limited degree; yet it would encourage them to fight the trend towards an increasingly partisan media.

Second, we could recognise the significance of public broadcasters as trusted facilitators of public debate in this new environment and increase their funding commensurately. That the ABC is the only media organisation which more than three-quarters of the public believes is fair and balanced, even today, is a testament to people's appreciation of the work of public broadcasters in the altered media environment.

Finally, because in the new networked public sphere all Australians will be both consumers and producers of content, we need to embed digital literacy and knowledge of citizenship in our children's education. This teaching would not only deal with the basics of evaluating information (how to judge whether a voice is reliable, how to spot a fraud), but also the responsible production and dissemination of information.

○

We should also be experimenting with the creation of new democratic institutions suited to the needs of contemporary Australia. Involving the public in the reform process gets a bad rap from political cynics, but it may be a valuable way of increasing the legitimacy of government. Imagine if a minister had a reform proposal that she knew would be a difficult sell. The proposal included complex facts and a range of trade-offs that could easily be distorted by vested interests and a fanatical media. The minister might welcome a democratic institution that allowed her to make her case in an environment where rules facilitating genuine deliberation were upheld. In a day-long session before a citizen jury of twenty randomly selected citizens—the kind of jury that's been used to evaluate the NDIS—the minister would not be able to persuade the participants through mere talking points alone. She would have to engage in a substantive policy debate to win the support of the group.

Shadow ministers could be allowed to put their own case to the jury, and a non-binding vote on the proposal from the jurors at the conclusion would bring genuine institutional legitimacy to the reforms. If the jury gave the proposal the seal of approval, the minister would be able to use this when making her case for the reform to the broader public. If the minister failed to convince the citizen jury within an institution designed for deliberation, it would be a strong message for her to take the proposed reform back to the drawing board.

The effectiveness of citizen juries depends substantially on their design. Those that can't prove independence from the government will look like window dressing. In the United Kingdom the hand of government on citizen juries was so heavy that some bemoaned the practice as being 'reduced to the standing of focus groups'. Citizen juries must also be transparent and accountable: it's important that recommendations are made available to the public. And they must be equal, not only in their gender and cultural make-up, but in their consideration of issues and in the spread of personalities across a group. Without this, citizen juries will be dismissed as just as ineffective as other forms of direct democracy.

We saw citizen juries' potential in Ireland's recent decision on marriage equality. The referendum that saw the Irish public vote nearly two to one in favour of equality began with a constitutional convention of sixty-six citizens randomly selected from the general public and thirty-three members of parliament from across the political spectrum. The convention was designed in close collaboration with experts in deliberative processes and created a space for structured debate that informed the ensuing referendum. It's true that other convention recommendations like lowering the voting age and lowering the age of eligibility to run for president have not yet succeeded at referendum in Ireland. But the fact that this process assisted a conservative Catholic nation which only legalised divorce in 1996 to implement a social change on the scale of marriage equality suggests that citizen juries possess real democratic power.

○

Participatory budgeting is another institutional innovation that gives citizens a direct say in the prioritisation of public spending, by allowing them to vote on which projects or programs proposed by the community should be supported by the government. It's an effective check on government for people sceptical about the necessity and independence of some public projects, and who see the failure of the government to install traffic lights at their local school as a reason to give up on their elected representatives altogether.

To date, participatory budgeting has largely occurred in municipal government: more than fifteen hundred local governments around the world have trialled the technique. In 2014 the mayor of Paris launched the biggest participatory-budgeting exercise yet, setting aside 5 per cent of the city's capital-investment budget for the next five years: over €400 million for projects voted on by the community. More than forty thousand Parisians voted, online and in person, on fifteen nominated projects.

There is no reason that the federal government here could not initiate a similar participatory-budgeting initiative to increase government responsiveness and public engagement. The government already supports a range of community and regional-development grant programs, and having local citizens rather than bureaucrats determining which projects and programs should be supported would be a logical next step. It's a tangible way for people to see the benefits of democratic engagement.

○

All of these measures will improve the health of our democratic institutions, but we also need to engage the Australian public in a project of continual democratic renewal. The cultural and technological change that has unfolded over the past twenty years will only accelerate in pace over the coming decades, and our institutions will have to continue to adapt in response to it. For many Australians, the way our democracy works feels immutable—set in stone by Henry Parkes and other men with long beards at the time of federation. The reality is very different. Australia has reaped the benefits of democratic innovation throughout its history. The problem is that Australians' understanding of how our system of government works is weak and their belief that the system itself can be changed is even weaker.

Teaching civics in Australian schools alone won't alter feelings of cynicism and powerlessness about the prospects for improving our democracy. We need an institutional framework that shows how change is possible and gives Australians who want change a goal to work towards. We've seen this first-hand with the republican movement. It's difficult to capture the public's attention for a cause with no finish line. But if you give reformers a goal to aim for—as Paul Keating did when, in 1995, he made it the policy of the government to seek an Australian republic by the centenary of federation, in

2001—you can capture public and media focus, and give impetus to community organising.

Australia should legislate for regular democratic-renewal conventions, comprising a mix of delegates elected directly via online and postal ballots, and delegates appointed by state and federal governments. In the lead-up to these conventions, to be held every ten years, we should conduct a series of online plebiscites to determine the issues that would be included on the convention's agenda, allowing advocacy groups to make the case for their issues to the public. The federal government should also be able to put issues on the agenda. This would create a forum for debates about important structural democratic reforms: for example, electoral funding and donations, reducing the voting age, fixed terms for the federal parliament, expanding the number of House of Representatives members and reducing the number of senators.

Australia has a proud history as a laboratory of democracy. There is perhaps no nation in the world with a longer history of experimentation with new models of representation. The Australia of the nineteenth and early twentieth centuries was an early pioneer of the universal franchise, the secret ballot, compulsory preferential voting, Saturday voting, pay for elected members, and abolishing wigs and gowns in parliament. Australia may be a young country in some respects, but it is an elder statesman in the field of democratic innovation. It's part of what made us successful throughout the twentieth century. So that our national good fortune does not run out over the next twenty-five years, we need to revive our great legacy of democratic innovation and experimentation, readying ourselves for the work of this century.

2

Inequality

AUSTRALIA'S NATIONAL STORY is unique. A bushranger who spoke poetically about social justice is celebrated, at once a criminal and a national hero. Young Australians have distinguished themselves in war not just for their grit and bravery, but for the easy egalitarian ways between officer and soldier. Our democratic tradition was founded by a motley crew of gold diggers: women and men, local and immigrant, patrician and proletariat, united in protest under the Southern Cross.

Through each of these foundation stories runs a common thread: equality. In Australia, we sit in the front seat of taxis. CEOs chat with junior staff in the lift. There is no hint of class when we talk with one another about the football or our children. But do these behaviours reflect a genuine balance of wealth? Do the facts accord with this celebrated aspect of our national identity?

The good news first: Australia is incredibly prosperous. As one of the richest nations in the world, we have a lot to share around. For each of the last twenty-four years, we have grown collectively wealthier. As our economy has grown, Australians across the income spectrum have, on average, seen their incomes increase. But, as the nation has become wealthier, it has also become less equal. While most Australians are sharing in our growing national prosperity, some are benefiting a great deal more than others.

The resulting distribution of wealth is out of whack with our national values. Today, the nine richest Australians control as much wealth as do the poorest four and a half million. In research commissioned by the ACTU in 2011, Australians were asked how they would like to see wealth distributed. Respondents wanted the top-fifth wealthiest households to control 24 per cent of national wealth; in reality, they control 61 per cent. Respondents wanted the bottom fifth to possess 15 per cent of national wealth; in reality, they possess just 1 per cent. Using income measures, Australia is today only the twenty-first most-equal nation in the OECD—behind Canada, Korea, Ireland, Poland, France, Luxembourg and fourteen other developed countries.

We want to live in a country where a child growing up in Springvale (in Clare's electorate) or Sunshine West (in Tim's) has just as good a chance as anyone to be a High Court judge or a CEO. Growing inequality jeopardises this possibility. Inequality is morally wrong, because who ends up wealthy and who ends up poor is only partly to do with merit. Ninety per cent of Australia's billionaires are pale and male. An Indigenous man is more likely to have a prison record than a university degree. A four-year-old living in a disadvantaged community is twice as likely to be developmentally vulnerable as a child in a wealthy one.

Inequality means human potential goes to waste—which, as well as being unjust, is bad for the economy. There is growing evidence for this from the hard-nosed, fact-driven economists at respected global institutions such as the International Monetary Fund (IMF) and the OECD. The existence of significant inequality usually leads to poorer-quality democracy, where people of tremendous wealth can buy positions on the boards of media companies or seats in parliament. And Australians rejected a bunyip aristocracy 160-odd years ago.

To understand why inequality in Australia is growing, what is set to happen to 2040 and what we can do about it, we need to consider how people attain their living standards. A person's quality of life can be assessed without explicit reference to their financial situation. Well-being, sense of community and happiness are important measures. But, for most people, money is a primary driver of quality of life. It affords choices, security and safety. And, unlike more abstract measures of well-being, it's readily quantifiable. So we will use income as the primary means of measuring inequality in this discussion. A person's income is derived from three possible sources: labour income from work, capital income such as rent or dividends from assets, and government income such as the aged pension.

Inequality debates are often framed around concerns about the accumulating wealth of the top 1 per cent of income earners. Australian evidence shows that while the top 1-per-centers are doing staggeringly well, they are not the main driver of increasing inequality in recent years. We are concerned with how to help the vast bulk of Australians adapt to a set of fundamental economic shifts that are underway, so they can share in the benefits of economic change rather than be victims of it. While many of our chapters are laced with caveats and uncertainties about the future, we are confident in this prediction: without policy change, by 2040 we will be living in a far more unequal Australia.

○

Many readers of this book will be Instagram users. For the uninitiated, Instagram is a social-media application you use to take photos on your phone and share them with friends. Today, Instagram has 300 million users and counting. Kodak, the photography company, had at its peak a 90 per cent share of the American film market and 145,000 employees. But in 2012 Kodak declared bankruptcy, a casualty of the Digital Revolution. Months later, Instagram was sold for one billion US dollars. The company had just thirteen employees.

Instagram is a commonly cited example of how technology and globalisation are changing the economics of work. Instagram's market is everyone in the world with an internet connection, and its cost of serving each additional customer is almost zero. And, ultimately, its vast economic rewards—which would once have shared wealth, through wages, across many thousands of workers—sit in the hands of a small number of founders and employees.

These trends are not just evident in upstart innovators like Instagram. Clare represents many manufacturers in Melbourne's southeast and she is a regular visitor to local factory floors. Most are teeming with activity. But the floor manager can often tell a story of a larger site, with more employees, when they started in the business. Today, robots are commonplace. Increasingly, instead of engaging with the process of manufacturing, workers are monitoring, assisting and fixing machines. In many of these businesses, profits are going up but the number of workers is going down.

At the lower-skill end of the labour market, jobs that cannot be outsourced or mechanised—such as food services and personal care—are growing in number. But conditions there are deteriorating, compared to those of average workers. The minimum wage has decreased as a share of the average wage—nearly 60 per cent in the early 1990s; less than 45 per cent today. Just under two-thirds of Australia's workers have paid annual leave and sick leave. More than a million workers are underemployed: they have some work, but want more and can't find it.

Australian families earn most of their income from wages. So anything that affects how wages are calculated and distributed is likely to have a big impact on inequality. Over the past thirty years, full-time workers on low incomes have seen modest improvement in their hourly wage, while those in higher income brackets have gone from strength to strength. In the late 1980s, wages of the top tenth of income earners were about five times larger than those in the bottom tenth; now they are about eight times larger.

Technology and globalisation are at the root of the problem. And the cycle is not new. Agriculture workers were replaced by farm machinery, manufacturers by robots. Now, those under threat are our paralegals and accountants. Who will be next? An Oxford University study predicted in 2013 that almost half the jobs that exist today in the United States will be replaced by machines within two decades.

The face of globalisation in the 1990s might have been a low-skilled Vietnamese textile worker who sewed mass production T-shirts for Gap. Today, it's a university-educated young person in India who develops PowerPoint presentations for management consultants working in New York or Nairobi, or a Filipino Telstra customer-service officer who manages complex complaints in perfect

English. By 2040, it could well be a radiographer with a world-class degree from a Chinese university who provides medical images to Australian customers from Beijing at a much lower price.

Global sourcing is bleeding into mainstream business, whether companies have two members of staff or two thousand. Take a look online at 99designs, where designers around the world compete to fulfil requests for new corporate branding. Or Fancy Hands, where an assistant can provide you with administrative support from any country in the world, at a fraction of the usual cost.

Australia's designers, customer-service staff, medical and many other professionals are, or soon will be, competing in a global labour market. For many, the pressure on wages will be downward. But not everyone will face this predicament. Those with highly valued skills—brilliant managers, dazzling creatives, tech-savvy wunderkinds who can write code or design machines—will reap huge rewards. The guys who started Instagram are multimillionaires. Some Kodak employees who lost their jobs when the company went bust have probably never worked again. Technology and globalisation are holding down wages and conditions at the bottom, and pushing them up at the top.

○

We began this chapter by noting that Australians on average, across all income levels, have seen their incomes grow over the last generation. How is this consistent with our tale of technology, global labour competition and diverging wages? To understand the conundrum, we examined the drivers of recent income growth in different households.

Over the last decade, the highest-earning group of Australian households have seen their income grow from $3,600 per week to $5,300 per week. Three-quarters of this growth has come from increased hourly wages, with the remaining quarter coming from greater capital income. The hours worked by people in these households declined slightly over the decade. They are getting paid more and working less.

In the lowest-earning households, Australians have also seen their incomes go up. But the main drivers of this growth have been increased government support and an increase to the number of hours being worked by people in those households. They are getting paid slightly more and working a lot more.

In principle, working more hours is a good thing. Work is important, and it remains the best way out of poverty that we know of. But its role in the inequality story is problematic, because we can only increase the hours people work—or the number of people in a household working—by so much. Once workforce participation peaks, labour income in the lowest-earning households is likely to grow very slowly, but wages in the top-earning households will continue to rise fast. And so will inequality—probably much more quickly than we have seen in recent years.

It's hard to estimate when we will reach our peak, because workforce participation depends on policy settings (for example, child-care subsidies directly affect the number of hours worked by Australian women). But, assuming we can increase participation to the levels currently seen in comparable countries such as Canada and New Zealand, we are looking at a fifteen- to twenty-year time horizon until we run out of road. By 2040, the problem of wage divergence is likely to be both much worse and more obvious. Inequality will get out of hand, very quickly.

○

While wages matter most of all to income inequality, there is another factor pushing up incomes for those at the top. Capital income is the money we derive from assets: rent from property, dividends from shares, interest from bank deposits. It constitutes only 10 per cent of total household income (compared to 80 per cent for labour income), and almost half of all Australians don't earn any capital income at all. But capital is likely to be an important driver of inequality by 2040.

The amount of capital being held to generate income is growing. Capital in high-income households is also delivering better returns than labour is in low-income households, so families who possess a lot of capital are seeing naturally higher income growth than those at the other end of the spectrum. And those who have the most capital are, in the main, already very wealthy.

Let's consider the two decades between 1992 and 2010. At both points the stock market (an important driver of capital income, as lots of capital ownership is held in shares) had started to recover following economic crises. The majority of Australians began and ended the period with almost no capital income. But the richest 5 per cent of Australians earned on average five hundred dollars a week in capital income in 1992, and more than triple that amount in 2010. That's impressive growth.

It is, however, dwarfed by the top 1 per cent, who saw their capital income triple to almost five thousand dollars per week by 2010. This is dwarfed again by the top 0.1 per cent, who in 2010 derived a whopping $22,000 per week from capital income. For these 24,000 Australians, almost three-quarters of their average weekly income is derived from what they own.

In *Capital in the Twenty-First Century*, the French economist Thomas Piketty used historical data from twenty countries to show that in a capitalist economy returns to capital will almost always grow faster than the economy itself. Piketty's findings—and the recent Australian experience—suggest that capital, as with labour income, is likely to play a more significant role in driving inequality in the years to 2040.

Housing is a distinctively Australian wrinkle in the capital story. Historically, home ownership here has not just been for the rich. Working-class families have bought the roof over their heads, seen their asset grow, and had an inheritance to pass on to their children.

But, over the last generation, housing prices have grown so fast that large numbers of young (and some not-so-young) Australians are getting locked out of the market. Research released in 2015 by the Grattan Institute showed that, in the early 1980s, more than 60 per cent of twenty-five- to thirty-four-year-olds owned a home. Now, the figure is under 50 per cent and falling. By far the biggest drop is among young people in the lowest-income bracket, who are now half as likely to own a home. Meanwhile, investors have increased their share, representing 25 per cent of the value of home loans in 1995 and 40 per cent by 2014. And 60 per cent of all investor-housing debt is held by Australians in the top fifth of income earners. Housing, once an equalising force, is becoming part of the inequality problem.

Declining home ownership among certain groups has been fuelled by high house prices, which have in turn been stoked by public policies: urban planning, limited land supply around our cities, increased population size through immigration, credit and negative gearing, to name a few.

The policy mix needs to change. Housing affordability disproportionately affects younger, lower-income people. Some of them tell us that facing a lifetime as renters is the single biggest issue influencing their quality of life. While each government policy alone may have a sound rationale, together they have unintended consequences. We need to increase the supply of affordable housing in our cities, help voters understand the links between higher-density urban development and housing affordability, and make a massive investment in public transport so that more parts of our cities are great places to live. And we need to wind back negative gearing. It's a tax break for investors that keeps house prices artificially high, young people out of the property market, and grows the wealth of the already wealthy.

o

How we collect taxes and distribute them through benefits (such as pension and unemployment payments) doesn't make for riveting dinner-party conversation. But without this kind of redistribution, many millions more Australians would live in poverty and our nation would be more unequal than Mexico, a land of shocking destitution and extreme wealth, of barrios and billionaires.

Historically, Australia's transfer system has done a good job of making our country fairer. Among OECD nations, Australia is one of the lowest spenders on welfare, but our spending has a big impact. Analysis from Professor Peter Whiteford at the Australian National University shows that Australia targets welfare spending at the people who need it most, and it does so better than almost any other country in the world. This, though, is a double-edged sword. It means that when we cut welfare, we cut the living standards of the poorest people in the country, and inequality rises, instantly.

The role of government in redistribution will continue to be contested over the coming decades. The nation faces a series of rising bills. Few will volunteer to pay more tax. For some politicians, cutting support to the most vulnerable will be the go-to response. But government benefits are the only way many Australians will ever get a slice of our growing national prosperity. When we cut family payments, pensions, support for the unemployed, or support for people with disability or illness, we reduce the living standards of the poorest people in Australia; and we make an explicit decision that, while the nation grows wealthier, some should be left behind. And that we are willing to live in a more unequal Australia.

Tax changes that advantage the wealthiest Australians have contributed greatly to rising inequality over recent years. We analysed how tax cuts over the last three decades affected a banker and a teacher. Assuming both were equally successful in their professions, in addition to earning a good deal more, the banker has been the great beneficiary of tax changes over this time. For every dollar gained from tax cuts by the teacher, the banker received about ten dollars in additional benefits. Research by the Australia Institute in 2013 had a similar finding: the top tenth of earners have gained more from tax cuts since 2005 than the bottom four-fifths combined.

So long as we're members of parliament we'll be drawn into regular debates about how to distribute the tax burden. In those debates, politicians should be mindful of the decades of rising systemic inequality that lie ahead. Tax changes, once made, are hard to unpick.

The federal budget is complex, and Australians cannot be expected to make sense of how different households will be affected by changes to our tax and transfer system. One practical change is for the federal government to release an inequality statement with each budget, explaining the impact of fiscal decisions on different households. We can then have a better-informed national debate about the effects of each budget on different groups of Australians and whether changes over time are fair.

○

Margaret Thatcher, the United Kingdom's prime minister from 1979 to 1990, was one of the world's first conservative leaders to apply free-market thinking in government. As opposition leader, Thatcher once became so fed up with the progressive direction of a colleague's presentation that she produced a copy of Friedrich Hayek's *The Constitution of Liberty* (a sort of free-market bible) from her handbag and slammed the book on the table, declaring, 'This is what we believe.'

Bob Hawke, a former union leader and Australia's prime minister from 1983 to 1991, pioneered economic policy reform alongside his treasurer and successor, Paul Keating. He was a Rhodes Scholar who'd sat on the board of the Reserve Bank. But, to many Australians, 'Hawkie' was the bloke who downed a yard glass of beer at world-record speed.

Both leaders presided over a period of immense economic transition that saw global trade boom, the service industries take off and the first personal computers appear in homes. Both governments came to power in periods of high unemployment and inflation, volatile industrial-relations disputes and economies that had grown lethargic under protectionist trade regimes. In response, both Hawke and Thatcher opened up their nations to trade and competition. But only Hawke realised that the resulting economic shift would require social policies designed to combat inequality.

Hawke pitched a consensus-driven industrial-relations system to the Australian public and, when elected, implemented the Prices and Incomes Accord, ending a long period of fractious industrial disputes. The concept of a social wage underpinned the accord, with union demands for pay rises moderated by the establishment of Medicare, a 19 per cent increase in the value of unemployment benefits relative to average wages and, later under Keating, the rollout of a compulsory superannuation scheme for workers. In addition, the government helped Australians understand what would be required of them in a changing economy. Over the life of the Hawke government, the number of students sticking with school to Year 12 rose from 40 to 71 per cent.

Thatcher took a different path. One of her first acts was to cut the link between social-security payments and wages, which saw unemployment benefits fall by a quarter relative to average earnings. As the United Kingdom's transfer system became less generous, tax changes made the tax system more regressive. Thatcher led a fierce assault on industrial-relations protections, with widespread strike action, and violent confrontations between police and unionists.

Over this period, the United Kingdom's child-poverty rate more than doubled, while income inequality skyrocketed. Hawke's policy prescriptions saw child poverty fall (though very slightly) and income inequality rise only marginally, bucking a global trend. Under Thatcher, the top 10 per cent saw their share of income rise by almost triple the rate seen in Australia under Hawke. By the time both governments left office, their countries were wealthier and more competitive. But the policy choices of the Hawke government had ensured the gains of the 1980s and early 1990s were spread across the community. Thatcher's belief that the newly created wealth would 'trickle down' never came to fruition.

Hawke and Keating believed that inequality was an important issue, and they did something about it. We believe inequality in Australia today is too high. We think that every Australian should have a fair go at making it to the top. That Australians should be rewarded for their creativity, talent and hard work. That all Australians, across the income spectrum, should have a dignified standard of living and share in our national prosperity.

○

In thinking through an agenda to tackle Australian inequality, we accept the economic shifts underway. We cannot control global forces; we cannot wind back the clock. Raising tariff walls, nationalising the banks and shutting out immigrants will not bring back the old Australia. Nor should we want it to. Economic growth over the last twenty-four years has raised the incomes of the least well-off Australians significantly. But growth can have sharp edges. Good policy is essential to making sure all Australians benefit.

The obvious place to start is to ensure that every Australian child gets a great education. Today, it's common at graduation ceremonies to see parents cheer wildly as the first member of their family receives a university degree. But, on average, the postcode you're born in and your parents' circumstances have a profound effect on your chances of educational success.

By Year 3, children with a university-educated parent are four times more likely to score in the top band of the national reading test than children whose parents didn't finish school. By the time Year 9 comes around, this proportion has swelled to twelve times. We see similar inequalities at the bottom end, where children from disadvantaged homes are vastly over-represented in the share who don't meet minimum standards and grow more over-represented as they progress through school. By the time school is finished, a young person from a high-income family is three times more likely to sit in a university lecture theatre than one from a low-income family. If we're relying on education to provide a level playing field for Australia's young people, these figures should give us pause for thought.

Gaps emerge early—they are evident on the first day of school—and there is a good deal of evidence that intervening in the early years is our best chance of getting young Australians on to an equal footing. A fast-growing body of knowledge about the development of the human brain supports this approach. The brain, like scaffolding, will only ever be as strong and stable as its foundations. Once laid, those foundations are difficult to shift. By the time they turn one, babies who hear only one language cannot recognise some sounds that don't occur in that language. That's why it's hard for native English speakers to perfect tonal languages, like Mandarin, later in life. Everything we go on to learn—counting to calculus, reading to rhetoric—builds on what we learn in the first years of life.

Professor James Heckman, an American early-childhood academic and Nobel laureate, has shown that for every year people grow older, inequality becomes more expensive to address. Returns on investment in the early years are significant—usually four to nine dollars returned for every dollar invested, and sometimes estimated to be as high as seventeen. (For context, if a major road project returns three dollars for every dollar spent, it is considered a runaway success.) In the fight against inequality, early learning gives us the biggest bang for buck.

A vast array of international studies show that high-quality early learning is strongly associated with better performance at school. Importantly, quality early learning gives the largest boost to the kids who are most disadvantaged. In studies testing the impact of quality early learning from infancy, such as the Carolina Abecedarian Project, participants have been shown to have higher IQs, stay longer in education and perform better on academic tests throughout their schooling.

The Perry Preschool Study is another famous early-learning study conducted in the United States. As adults, the Perry Preschool children were much less likely to be in trouble with the law, and more likely to be on high incomes, own their own home and to have graduated from high school. The impacts persisted, forever.

High-quality early learning is not just about children getting to grips with their ABCs. Program benefits go beyond academic success, because quality early learning improves non-cognitive skills: how to listen and respond to instructions, resolve conflict, make friends, work in a group, feel good about learning and exercise the beginnings of self-control and discipline. When children begin school with these foundations already in place, they are more likely to develop good relationships with peers and teachers, enjoy school, and learn more easily.

Broadly speaking, quality early learning means educators with good training in early-years education, centres with low staff-to-child ratios, language-rich environments (lots of books, lots of conversation), and warm, encouraging relationships between educators and kids. Many successful programs also get families involved, whereby parents are supported to fulfil their role as their child's first teachers.

In recent years, Australia has significantly improved the accessibility and quality of early-years education. The vast majority of Australian children now attend preschool from age four. But world leaders in early education achieved this some time ago, and now the goalposts have shifted. In France, Sweden, Denmark and Belgium early education is effectively universal at age three. New Zealand enrols 90 per cent of three-year-olds in twenty hours a week of free early learning. Britain has near-universal enrolment of three-year-olds through fifteen hours of free early learning, and is extending this to two-year-olds in low-income families. Meanwhile, a measly 18 per cent of Australian three-year-olds are enrolled in early learning (though more are in formal child care), ranking thirty-fourth out of the thirty-seven OECD nations.

This is particularly problematic because the Australian children most likely to miss out on early learning are those who need it most. Children who are Indigenous, live in a remote or low-income community, or have non-English-speaking parents or a single parent are less likely to access early learning. Children from disadvantaged families and communities who are enrolled are more likely to get a lower quality of care.

Australian early education is beset by a number of other problems, including high fees, long waiting lists, poor pay and limited recognition of early-childhood educators. Fixing these problems will be expensive, but it will benefit the nation. We've already mentioned the incredible return on investment by helping children to reach their full potential as adults. More accessible, high-quality early learning will also lead to greater workforce participation by women. In 2000 the Quebec provincial government decided to offer high-quality preschooling to every child for five dollars a day. It was an expensive outlay, but the cost was fully recovered through the increased tax paid by women who were able to do more paid work because of the program.

High-quality, universal early learning is a rare piece of public policy where the aims of all Australian political parties intersect: it's good for children, families, women; a powerful driver of economic growth. And it's the best weapon against intergenerational inequality that we know of. So it's not a question of whether we can afford to make the changes we need. It's a question of whether we can afford not to.

○

Educational opportunity is heavily shaped by parenting and what goes on at home. By the time children are eighteen months old, disparities in vocabulary between those growing up in high- and low-income households are already apparent. In the 1970s two American academics, Betty Hart and Todd R. Risley, set out to explain why. By measuring the words spoken to children in different households, they found that, by age four, a child in a high-income household had heard thirty million more words than a child in a disadvantaged household. For disadvantaged families, quality early learning combined with effective parenting support is the best way to get kids off to a good start.

Almost all parents want to be great parents. But some have to manage extra worries: poverty, homelessness, insecure income, family violence, disability and illness. They need extra support, and we have to find a way to provide it without prying or being judgmental.

One straightforward solution is providing accessible information. The American professor of education Meredith L. Rowe has shown that one reason why disadvantaged American parents spoke to their children less than, and differently from, other parents was simply a knowledge gap: they hadn't realised how important talking with children was to language development. In a 2008 study, Rowe further reported that low-income parents were more likely to get information about parenting from friends and relatives, whereas high-income parents were going to the doctor, reading books about child development and talking to experts.

A local success story is the Home Interaction Program for Parents and Youngsters (HIPPY), run in Australia by the Brotherhood of St Lawrence. HIPPY is interventionist, working intensively with families by providing home tutoring and family support. The program brings children who are about one-third below average in reading and writing as four-year-olds up to average level within two years: a remarkable achievement. But programs like these operate at the margins; in 2014, HIPPY serviced seventy-five Australian communities. The results suggest significant scope for expansion.

Most of the studies and much of the evidence we refer to are from the United Kingdom or the United States. Critical readers may have legitimate questions about whether the findings apply to Australia. There has been too little experimentation with, and too little evaluation of, different policy options in Australian early-years policy. For example, Australia has never conducted a truly rigorous study of early learning in Indigenous communities.

What's the best way to interact with families? What does school readiness look like, and how do we teach it? Where does home visiting fit in? We need to build a better culture—within government and outside of it—to start finding the answers to these critical questions, and building a larger community of policy experts who will help to ensure that all Australian children get off to a good start.

A British study has shown that, for disadvantaged children, the quality of their eighteen months of preschool education is more important in determining reading levels at Year 5 than the quality of their primary school. Yet so much of our education debate in Australia is dominated by primary education. To tackle the problems we've discussed, early-years policy needs to rise quickly to the top of the agenda and stay there. Having a cabinet minister with overall responsibility for Australian children would help to make it happen.

○

Even with the best parenting and early-childhood education, not all Australians will end up on an academic track—and that's okay. The nation wouldn't function without aged-care workers and electricians, construction workers and restaurateurs. But these workers, too, will fare better in the coming decades if they are better educated. Lindsay Fox and Paul Keating could make it without finishing high school, but those days are behind us. Opportunities for people without basic skills are increasingly rare, and job quality for those without them is deteriorating.

In helping to secure basic skills for our young people, Australia lags behind the top-performing countries. The share of young people gaining a Year 12 qualification in Australia has improved over the last decade, but slowly, with about one in five not making it through. In top-performing countries, nine in ten students complete Year 12. These national averages mask areas of deep concern. Only four in ten low-income Tasmanian students finish high school the first time around. In very remote parts of the Northern Territory, just two in ten do.

The renowned education expert Professor John Hattie at the University of Melbourne points out that, if we want students to stick with learning for as long as they can, school has to be an inviting place for all kinds of young people. For some young people who aren't academic, school can make them feel like a failure, every day.

In Victoria, a charity called Hands On Learning Australia takes small groups of students in Years 7 to 10 out of the classroom for one day a week to build things that are needed by their school community. The program helps young people to discover what they're good at, and emphasises teamwork, leadership and a sense of belonging. Hands On Learning has massively reduced detention and unemployment rates for its participants. And it has helped raise the school retention rate for a group of high-risk young people to 95 per cent.

Everton Park State High School in Brisbane's north is blazing a trail in supporting young people headed for vocational education. The curriculum between Years 7 and 9 has much in common with other Queensland schools. In Year 10 students get the chance to complete two work-experience stints, as well as a mentoring program that helps them decide whether to follow the conventional academic path or a vocational one. For those who choose the latter, roughly half of their time is spent taking Vocational Education and Training (VET) courses and gaining work experience. A typical student on this pathway will finish Year 12 with certificates in business and hospitality, as well as having completed a traineeship in a child-care centre.

By 2040, Australia's economy will demand many more Australians with higher skills, and relatively fewer without a qualification. Many Australians will do their post-secondary training in our VET system, including a significant share of low-income students. The state of the VET system is therefore a critical inequality issue for Australia. It's also an essential economic issue. Jobs with technical-skill requirements—complex-machinery operation, design, digital media—aren't going away. Many aspects of our VET system work effectively, but there are also well-documented issues: students graduating without the skills they paid for, unscrupulous operators providing shoddy qualifications, young people racking up debt for training that may never lead to employment.

There is an obvious and urgent need for better oversight of the sector. But reforms should go beyond this. We need to push VET training into workplaces sooner, and for longer, so that early on students get a realistic view of what they're being trained for and gain basic work experience while they learn. Some VET providers continue to be too far removed from industry: we need to find more innovative ways to connect employers with providers. And we must improve the guidance offered to Australians, so that they can make well-informed plans for their careers and good decisions about further study. We want careers counselling to be available to any person at a transition point in their career. Australians should have ready access to current information about the skills needs in their region, independent advice about options for training, and realistic appraisals of employment opportunities that may be available at the end of their course.

o

We are not typical of Labor MPs in some ways. Neither of us has ever worked for a union, and we have spent more time in boardrooms than on shop floors. But we recognise that as our economy modernises unions are becoming more, not less, important to tackling inequality.

Historically, the IMF is one of the most conservative finance-research organisations in the world—hardly the bastion of radical collectivism. In 2015 two IMF researchers, Florence Jaumotte and Carolina Osorio Buitron, examined the drivers of inequality in countries around the world. Their core finding was that in countries with high rates of unionism prosperity is much more equally shared.

Their study showed that declining unionism explains about half of the increase in inequality in some countries.

Unions get a hard time in Australia. Yet they are responsible for the eight-hour day and our minimum-wage system. They have led the fight for superannuation, paid parental leave and equal pay for women. They have a legitimate, important role that needs to be respected.

Today, unions face a lot of challenges. The shift in our economy away from blue-collar industries, the greater prevalence of small business, the rise of insecure work and changes to industrial-relations laws are undermining the traditional model of organising workers. A small number of unions give the sector a bad name, bolstering efforts by conservatives to portray unionism as a relic. Today, only 17 per cent of Australian employees are trade-union members, with rates at 12 per cent in the private sector. Membership was as high as 40 per cent in the early 1990s.

Given the importance of unions as a check to inequality, it goes without saying that we should fight attempts to restrict the right of workers to organise. But some unions are moving beyond this traditional territory, playing a role in a civil society that affects the quality of life of their members just as much as what goes on at work does. Community unionism has been adopted by the National Union of Workers, allowing Australians from all walks of life to sign up and play a role in the fight for social justice, for one dollar a week. Other unions are participating actively in public-policy debates, using social media to expose workplace exploitation, and fighting inequality head-on in political forums and media. Partnerships between unions and other groups with similar aims are already common overseas. In East London, forty organisations—including local churches, unions, schools and hospitals—have joined together to campaign for better living wages in their local services economy.

Organising workers to share ownership of capital through co-operatives is another area with promise. Mondragon, in Spain, is a conglomerate of 250 companies that is run by its employees. During the 2008–09 financial crisis, in return for higher levels of job security relative to the rest of the beleaguered Spanish economy, workers at Mondragon decided to accept postponed or slightly lower wages, lower dividends or temporarily lower hours.

Co-operatives haven't taken off to this degree here (with notable exceptions such as Murray Goulburn, the farmer-owned national icon that processes a third of Australia's milk supply). State and territory co-operative laws have recently been harmonised, so the environment for co-operatives is becoming more favourable. Unions, with their organising power, are the logical co-ordinators of Australian co-operatives. The emerging sharing economy, where people offer services through Uber, Airbnb and Airtasker, raises additional issues for unions (how can you organise workers who don't have an employer?), yet it also presents opportunities. A New Jersey trade union has helped launch a co-operative like Uber, but which is owned and run by its drivers.

Co-operative models are not going to solve Australia's inequality problem, and they shouldn't detract from the core business of unions: organising workers to bargain for quality jobs that provide a fair standard of living. But, given the drivers of inequality we've outlined above, co-operative models seem like a logical direction, offering the prospect of a broader distribution of capital.

o

We have argued that capital income is a growing part of the inequality problem because an increased share of Australia's prosperity is flowing to holders of capital. Our tax system is exacerbating this problem. Today, more than a third of superannuation tax concessions go to the top tenth of income earners. That same group yields approximately 70 per cent of capital-gains concessions and one-third of negative-gearing concessions. These federal policies provide far more preferential treatment to the dollars earned from capital than to the dollars that workers earn from labour.

Imagine two people earning eighty thousand per year. One receives his money in wages and owns no investment properties; for every additional dollar he earns, he pays one-third in tax. The other gets her income from capital: superannuation, share dividends and rent from several investment properties. Her super earnings attract only 15 per cent tax, and her investment properties attract further perks. Negative-gearing entitlements mean tax on income from shares or rent can be offset using interest payable on loans for investment properties. Expenses on the properties can also be used to further deduct tax. And if she decides to sell a property, she'll receive a 50 per cent discount on the tax she would've paid if she'd earned the same money through wages.

Combined, federal concessions on superannuation, negative gearing and capital gains constituted around forty billion dollars in 2013–14. This is roughly the cost of the aged pension. We need to take a clear-eyed view of how capital income is taxed in Australia and consider whether there are policy justifications for each tax break.

In addition, there's a global conversation underway about how taxes on capital itself (a tax calculated on an individual's assets, rather than on the income earned from them) could help manage growing inequality and revenue problems. We're not in favour of or against such a proposal: our tax system faces much bigger problems with clearer solutions. But what principles would we use to assess whether such a tax should be considered in Australia?

First, those who have considerable means to contribute towards the public good should contribute. Second, social mobility is important and inheritance can entrench inequalities across generations. Third, people have a legitimate desire to save and to pass on inheritances to their children, and they should not be penalised for doing that. In Clare's electorate, many first-generation migrant families commit their lives to ensuring that their children will be more financially secure than they were—and there's nothing wrong with that. And finally, a reality check: we face global competition to attract and retain talented people in Australia. We shouldn't create a tax system that deters wealthy people from living in our country.

○

In 2010 Clare lived in North East Arnhem Land, working in an Aboriginal community that continues to live by traditions of land and culture that have survived for thousands of years, yet is beset by crises in health, housing and employment. Australia can never be what it wants to be—a proud country, strong, diverse—until this national shame is addressed.

There have been some improvements over the last decade. The life-expectancy gap between Indigenous and other Australians has narrowed slightly, mortality rates for Indigenous children are falling, and more Indigenous young people are completing Year 12. Today, Indigenous Australians with a post-secondary education have similar employment outcomes to their non-Indigenous peers with the same qualification. But there are still many areas where we are standing still, and some where we are going backwards.

One of the toughest challenges in developing and implementing Indigenous policy is that it's impossible to generalise. The experiences of First Australians across the nation are worlds apart. Even communities separated by a few kilometres have different histories and different troubles: some are vibrant, with a rich connection to traditional culture; others have a history of political activism. Some are plagued by alcohol; some are peaceful communities, where the quality of life is high. We cannot scoop up the experiences of a Koori person in Melbourne and a young person living in the shadow of Uluru and see their situations as one and the same.

Governments thrive on programs designed for big problems with clear boundaries, where rules can be applied, criteria can be met and one size fits all. But each Indigenous community has different views, different challenges and different resources with which to confront the future. So our public policy for Indigenous Australians is going to have to be more agile, more targeted, more empathetic. We're seeing some success around Australia where community leaders have taken control.

The Cape York Welfare Reform scheme has demonstrated some positive early results by balancing rights with individual responsibilities, though there's still much work to be done. Cape York's Family Responsibilities Commission (FRC) works with people who receive welfare payments or work on Community Development Employment Projects and who fail to send their children to school, or receive a conviction, or breach a tenancy agreement. Depending on each individual's circumstances, the FRC can impose income management: a proportion of a person's income is set aside for essentials. To complement the FRC's emphasis on individual accountability, residents in the Cape are offered support, including financial-management services, educational-savings trusts and parenting programs. Although the Cape still lags behind most of Australia, particularly in employment outcomes, evaluations suggest the system of local leadership is working.

When Clare lived in Arnhem Land, visits from politicians and bureaucrats were a nice opportunity for a charade. People in neatly pressed chinos would fly into the searing heat. The locals would put on uniforms that hadn't been worn in months, lining up for photos. And when the politicians left in the evening, everything went back to normal. Some of the kids stopped going to school; some of the adults stopped going to work and training. The Aboriginal people used to call these visitors 'plastic bags'—because they would blow in, shake around and make a lot of noise, then get blown out of town again.

The reforms in Cape York and other emerging successes, such as the Living Change program in the East Kimberley, have at least one aspect in common—local Indigenous leaders, with a permanent commitment to the local area, have worked with their community to take ownership of problems and to find solutions. When future plans are created for other communities, they must come from the leadership of First Australians.

But how can we expect Aboriginal Australians to lead their communities when Canberra has removed many of their rights to self-govern? While land councils continue to play an important role, the Aboriginal and Torres Strait Islander Commission was abolished a decade ago. True, there were serious problems with aspects of community leadership, including corruption. But when we see these problems in non-Indigenous communities, we don't shut down democracy. First Australians need their own recognised leaders and their own form of self-government, and we should help to facilitate that.

More emphasis should be placed on the role of women and girls in Indigenous Australia. Work by the World Bank and other international-development organisations has consistently shown that investing in women creates positive ripple effects, improving the health and welfare of the whole community. This fundamental principle informs Australia's overseas-development program, yet it has not permeated our domestic policy. Indigenous woman face extraordinarily high levels of domestic violence, are far more likely to bear children in their teens and are significantly less likely than their male counterparts to participate in the workforce. There are renowned education initiatives for boys—such as the Clontarf Program, which uses football to keep 3,700 boys in school. Indigenous girls deserve similar large-scale programs.

Last, reconciliation really matters. Aboriginal people want to feel proud of their culture: that where they come from and who they are is recognised. We need to recognise Indigenous Australians in the nation's constitution. This must be pursued with support from all sides of politics. Then, we need to take advice from Indigenous Australians, and together chart a course to the next wave of legal and constitutional reforms that will appropriately recognise their role as the First Australians and the history that has followed.

○

For a brief time in the nineteenth century, Australia was the most prosperous nation in the world and known as 'the working man's paradise'. The colonies had thrown off Britain's stifling class strictures: in our land, Jack was as good as his master.

But, in the years before federation, Australia slipped into depression. Unemployment was widespread. There was no social safety net; no Medicare, no minimum wage. Many Australians lived in shanties, in the kind of distressing poverty that most of us today see only on television.

Federation was in part an expression of collective hope: that Australians' sense of egalitarianism could and should be reflected economically. In the decades that followed, good women and men—from Edith Cowan to John Curtin, Enid Lyons to Vincent Lingiari, Vida Goldstein to Gough Whitlam, Henry Bournes Higgins to Fred Hollows—fought inequality in different corners of the nation. Some battles they won. Others are still underway.

There is a growing chasm between Australians' oft-expressed desire to live as a fair and equal society and the reality of life in our country. By 2040, that chasm will almost certainly widen. If we are serious as a nation about living out our values, policy will have to change, substantially and fast. Helping the vast majority of Australians to benefit from the economic changes on the horizon is a huge challenge. But the nation has faced—and overcome—bigger ones.

3

Technology

IN OUR HYPE-DRIVEN, marketing-soaked world, we're used to hearing empty claims about the ways our lives are being revolutionised. Yet we shouldn't allow healthy cynicism to cloud the fact that we are living through a revolution that is fundamentally reshaping our institutions, our economy and our government. The Digital Revolution, the combination of digitisation and widespread connectivity, is changing the way people interact, the way machines interact, and the way people and machines interact.

These changes are helping people to access a wider range of goods and services at lower prices. They are creating openings for businesses to access global markets, adopt new models, and make use of currently wasted human and infrastructure capacity. And they are offering a means for governments to meet the shifting expectations of their citizens, by harnessing the power of online communities and by drawing new insights from the oceans of data about our world that are being produced behind the scenes every day.

But they also mean that Australian businesses will have to work hard to be revolutionaries, rather than road kill, during this period of change. Governments will need creatively to build an environment that enables Australians to enjoy the benefits of digital disruption. Educators, employers and communities alike will need to alter the ways in which they operate to ensure that Australian workers have the opportunity to be a part of the Digital Revolution.

We're not technological determinists. We don't believe that technological innovation sets our society on a single, unwavering path. We'll see enormous technological innovation over the coming decades, but it will be our values and how they guide the decisions we make that will determine what our society looks like in 2040.

○

Human interaction is fundamental to our institutions and businesses, our governments and communities. It's the basis of almost everything we do. And the Digital Revolution is reshaping our society by altering the ways in which we interact with one another—how we learn and create, how we work and socialise.

The Nobel Prize-winning economist Ronald Coase has argued that we organise our interactions with other people largely by the costs of doing things with them. Transaction costs can include the costs of finding people, gathering enough information to judge whether they're worth working with, setting the terms under which they work together, and monitoring and enforcing those terms. They're the reason why for the past century many of our interactions with other people occurred within, or between, a particular kind of organisation. The sociologist Max Weber described the typical twentieth-century organisation as a hierarchical, siloed, rules-based bureaucracy, populated by individuals permanently engaged to perform specific tasks: government departments, companies, law firms, hospitals, schools. These Weberian organisations still dominate our lives.

However, as the Harvard professor Yochai Benkler has identified, the transaction costs that shaped many of those organisations and institutions have now collapsed, thanks to the Digital Revolution. It's never been easier to find like-minded people, share information with them, and collaborate across time and space to achieve a shared goal. It's now possible to have non-hierarchical organisations that rely on small contributions from huge numbers of transient contributors.

At the community level, the costs of interaction are now so low that we're seeing the organic formation of a new type of group, one dedicated to niche concerns which could never have supported formal organisations in the past. In Tim's electorate, in Melbourne's west, a plethora of online groups have sprung up, through which people with similar interests help each other in small, everyday ways. The 2,200 members of the Inner West Mums and Bubs group organise meet-ups and playdates, and share tips about local playgrounds and child-care centres, schools and family activities. The 4,600 members of the West Welcome Wagon group collect donations of food and homewares to put together welcome packs for local asylum seekers, and provide ongoing material and social support to the community. The Altona Loop Group lets locals warn each other about delays and cancellations on the local train line; its members also lobby local political representatives for improvements—both online and through debates attended by the representatives.

Before the Digital Revolution, finding people with these shared interests would have involved canvassing the community, posting flyers and taking out ads in the local paper. Once these people had found each other, doing anything as a group would have demanded a significant commitment of time and resources for discussion and decision-making. Because the costs of finding and connecting with people online are minimal, these groups can emerge swiftly and easily. Thousands of quick interactions that provide small but tangible benefits are now occurring around the clock, locally and globally.

o

In the business sector, the collapse of transaction costs has had profound effects. The organisational theory pioneered by Ronald Coase and others holds that the structures of companies will largely be determined by how hard it is to interact with others. As the Digital Revolution has shrunk those costs of interaction, the boundaries of businesses have contracted and blurred. When the costs of doing business with people outside your company fall dramatically, it makes sense to outsource work to specialists who are experts in tasks that are becoming ever more niche.

As we discussed in the Inequality chapter, the greater speed and reliability of communication have also internationalised employment markets, making the costs for a Sydney-based business of contracting someone in Colombo comparable to those for someone in Canberra. Lower interaction costs are not only affecting our business structures; they're reshaping our employment markets, as increased specialisation reduces job security and puts downward pressure on wages.

It's now so easy to interact with others that a new business model has emerged which effectively turns companies inside out. In this model, companies 'employ' far more individuals outside the firm than inside it. The sharing economy, or collaborative consumption, sees companies centralise basic functions like payment systems, marketing and complaints resolution under a prominent consumer brand. They then rely on huge numbers of individuals outside the firm to provide services directly offered to customers. Money passes from customer to provider, with the company taking a cut of the price for enabling the transaction.

These are major businesses that are reshaping significant sectors of our economy. Take Airbnb, which many readers will be familiar with. It provides an online platform that verifies the identity of property owners and lets them offer space in their properties for short-term rental. The business is reportedly worth ten billion US dollars, yet it doesn't own any properties itself. In the past such a distributed accommodation model would have been impossible, because it would have been too hard and costly to manage so many interactions with so many people. But Airbnb takes advantage of the lower costs of finding, evaluating and contracting with people online to make use of existing infrastructure that was previously wasted—all those spare rooms. Airbnb now offers more than a million listings across 34,000 cities and 190 countries. Over 420,000 people use it on a peak night, and Airbnb hosted an estimated one-fifth of all attendees of the 2014 FIFA World Cup in Brazil. It's the official 'alternative accommodations' sponsor of the 2016 Olympics. Australia even has an Airbnb MP: Tim uses the service to find accommodation when he's in Canberra for parliamentary sittings.

These peer-to-peer business models have already disrupted the existing markets for banking (PayPal, Venmo), fundraising (Pozible, Kickstarter, GoFundMe), second-hand goods (eBay, craigslist), crafts (Etsy), transport (Uber, Lyft, Sidecar, GoGet), freelance services (Fiverr, Freelancer), data analysis (Kaggle) and education (Coursera, edX). Some Australian companies are adopting open business models of this kind, most notably Freelancer, Kaggle and 99designs; but, at present, there are more Australian businesses whose markets are being disrupted than there are those doing the disruption.

The Digital Revolution hasn't just changed the way people interact within the community and business sectors; it's also created new ways for communities and businesses to collaborate. We've seen an entirely new form of production emerge that relies not on profits, but on passion. Peer production is dependent on the voluntary contributions of large numbers of individuals within an online community (some amateur, some professional) to produce what the Australian economist Nicholas Gruen calls 'emergent public goods'. Nowhere is the power of this phenomenon better illustrated than by Wikipedia, the online community that harnesses the voluntary contributions of around twenty-three million passionate amateurs. It has produced more than thirty million articles in 287 languages that in total are viewed more than twenty billion times a month.

Online communities of this kind are already becoming productive resources for our communities, businesses and governments. While technological advances get most of the attention, at the most basic level it is the human interaction facilitated through the machinery of online communities that is the most important part of the Digital Revolution. As the anthropologist Michael Wesch puts it, in this new age of mass digital connectivity 'The Machine Is Us/ing Us'.

○

Just as the Digital Revolution has made it easier for humans to interact, it's also made it easier for machines to interact with other machines. This machine-to-machine interaction has created a new digital realm to our lives, in which data about our actions is recorded, aggregated and stored. The twin phenomena of digitisation and connectivity, combined with falling costs of computer processing and data storage, have led to an explosion in the volume of data about our world being collected, analysed and shared by machines. IBM has estimated that, in 2012, 2.5 exabytes of data was being generated around the world in just one day. You could try to conceive of that much data by imagining all the songs, photos and texts on more than forty-two million 64GB iPhones being created anew every day…though, unless you're a numbers geek, even that probably wouldn't mean much!

The scale of this data will only grow in the future, as internet-connected sensors permeate the way we move (cars, roads, tolls, rail carriages), the places we live (power points, taps, fridges, thermostats) and even how we live (wearables, pedometers, health monitors). Scientists are already experimenting with prototypes of skin-adhesive temporary tattoos that are able to track an individual's blood-glucose levels in real-time.

This is why the world is adopting a new registration system, IPv6, that allows for 340 trillion trillion trillion IP addresses: we were exhausting the total number of addresses that could be given to people and objects under the existing system which we use to locate things on the internet. The emergence of this internet of things will mean that, over the coming decades, not only will everyone around us be connected to the internet: so too will everything.

Advances in processing power and machine learning have enabled computers to identify patterns and connections within and between these new data sets, forming insights that are beyond the capabilities of human analysis. The transformation of this data into applications and services that can be used by people and businesses, like Google Maps complete with traffic data, has similarly huge potential. It's the big new resource of the twenty-first century, and we're all making it ourselves.

This data should offer insights into the efficiency of the way we run our businesses and our governments. However, as more economic and social activities become digitised, more of our lives will be subject to direct monitoring and potential control. In this new world we will need constantly to confront fresh and serious threats to our privacy, dignity and security.

○

The third major change brought about by the Digital Revolution is that it has created new ways for humans and machines to interact, with profound implications for the future of employment. In the coming decades the Digital Revolution will take a pincer grip on the Australian employment market, squeezing both low-skilled and high-skilled jobs.

In the low-skilled segment of the workforce self-service technology has proliferated, both online and in the physical world. Tasks that were once performed by low-skilled workers are being carried out by customers interacting with machines: at ATMs, on toll roads, at supermarket checkouts, in movie theatres, on public transport and at airport check-ins. These are all services that used to come with a human smile (usually, anyway), not a robotic swipe—and the trend has a long way yet to run.

According to the International Federation of Robotics, a record 178,132 industrial robots were sold worldwide in 2013. In the transport sector, Rio Tinto's Mine of the Future project has fifty-three 'autonomous trucks' moving ore in its Pilbara mines; Rio's AutoHaul long-distance driverless railway begins operation this year. Entrepreneurs are working on plans for crewless container ships and pilotless planes. And it's not difficult to imagine Google's prototype self-driving cars taking the jobs of taxi drivers and couriers in the coming decades. Uber CEO Travis Kalanick has already expressed his company's desire to replace its drivers with a fleet of self-driving cars in the future. Given that almost six hundred thousand Australians currently work in transport-related roles, there are significant consequences for our future employment patterns.

Machines are also threatening to replace humans in high-skill professional sectors. Computers are now being used for more than just computational data processing. They're being taught to recognise patterns and derive meaning from them, which has led to the emergence of machine-assisted professional services: pilots flying with the assistance of flight computers, doctors and nurses using algorithm-assisted diagnosis, lawyers performing legal-document reviews using computer algorithms instead of graduates and clerks.

None of these jobs will be completely automated. Nobody is going to develop a full-service robot nurse or lawyer—at least, not this century. However, these tools do have the potential dramatically to improve the productivity of experienced, high-skill professionals. That will reduce overall demand for human labour in these roles, particularly for those workers who haven't yet had the opportunity to develop their skills—not a rosy prospect for current students in these areas.

The Digital Revolution will undoubtedly destroy existing jobs, but it's not all doom and gloom—for it will also create new ones. Though John Maynard Keynes infamously warned of the possibility of mass unemployment as a result of 'our discovery of means of economising the use of labour outrunning the pace at which we can find new uses for labour', this hasn't been the outcome of previous technological revolutions.

According to census data, in 1911 more than a quarter of the Australian population was employed in the agricultural sector. A century later, technological innovation and productivity gains have reduced the number of Australians working on the land to just 2.5 per cent of our total workforce, and we haven't faced an unemployment apocalypse. Instead, cheaper agricultural goods have meant that consumers spend less money on food, in turn creating more demand for manufactured goods and, as a result, the labour required to produce them. Similar changes in supply and demand have occurred in the manufacturing and services economies in recent decades. Twenty years ago, nobody would have imagined that a person could be employed as a 'social media community manager', a 'search engine optimiser', or a 'CRM developer', but the Digital Revolution is creating jobs like these all the time.

Yet, just as exposing the Australian economy to domestic and international competition in the 1980s and 1990s caused significant employment restructuring, so too will the Digital Revolution precipitate structural change in the coming decades. Without government action, the Digital Revolution could hollow out the Australian employment market through an accelerated form of what economists call 'skill-biased technological change': the replacement of existing low-skilled jobs with new higher-skilled jobs.

Many of these jobs will demand digital literacy well beyond the skill set of the bulk of our current workforce. The American economist Tyler Cowen estimates that a small number of highly skilled individuals (maybe one in ten) will be able to interact with machines to significantly increase their productivity and reap enormous gains.

Many more middle-income jobs will be eradicated by technology and these workers could be forced into low-wage, insecure roles.

o

Business, too, will face big changes as a result of the Digital Revolution. Digitisation and widespread connectivity are general-purpose technologies: technologies that affect all segments of the economy, as the steam engine, railroads and electricity did in the past.

Deloitte sought recently to evaluate the potential impact of the Digital Revolution in Australia. It found that one-third of the economy will experience a dramatic change in revenues within three years, including sectors such as information and communications technology (ICT) and media, retail trade, arts and recreation, real estate, professional services and finance. The report predicted that a further third of the economy will experience dramatic changes over the longer term, including the education, health, transport and post, agriculture, utilities and government-services sectors. This change is inevitable. If Australian businesses do not bring the Digital Revolution to their own markets, a travel start-up from Finland, a robotics company from Hong Kong or a health-services provider from the United States will bring it instead.

By enabling low-cost interaction across time and space, cheap replication of digital goods and efficient scaling of services, the Digital Revolution has created globalised markets for many products and services. Putting governmental barriers to trade aside for a moment, the potential market for Australian businesses and the potential returns to be made on their products are much larger than they were twenty years ago.

It's never been easier for Australian businesses and entrepreneurs to create global brands. One of our favourite examples of this new dynamic is Natalie Tran. The daughter of Vietnamese refugees, Natalie has built a global following from Western Sydney. She's attracted over 1.7 million subscribers to her YouTube channel (communitychannel) and 540 million views of her uniquely Australian observational comedy and skits. In 2010 TubeMogul listed her as one of the world's ten-biggest independent earners from YouTube advertising.

In a similar way, Freelancer, a Sydney-based online marketplace linking freelance workers with employers, was able to grow to fourteen million users and seven million projects worth more than $2.5 billion in just five years, becoming the largest marketplace of its kind in the world. This is what's possible when the costs of delivering your goods and services to the world are so low.

There is a catch. While Australians can now sell their products to almost anyone in the world, consumers can also choose to buy from any provider, anywhere. Australian businesses don't merely have many more competitors. They need to be among the best in the world just to survive—there's no longer a market for an inferior domestic equivalent of a global offering. The Digital Revolution has created a plethora of 'superstar markets': winner-takes-all economies in which a small number of perceived high-quality providers command a premium. Can you name the fourth-best search engine in the world?

○

How Australia responds to the Digital Revolution depends on us as a community, not on what the tech geeks invent next. While technological change is inevitable, its consequences for our society are not. Digitisation and connectivity allow us to collect data that could change our understanding of the world, and collaboration that could change the way we interact in business, government and the community, but the impact they have on Australia is up to all of us. Governments play a major role in realising the full potential of new technologies and minimising the attendant risks.

The best way to realise the benefits of the Digital Revolution is to try to maximise the online interactions underpinning new opportunities: to work with the dynamics of change rather than against them. This requires an open online environment with as few regulatory barriers as possible. But government will still need to be involved—both in setting boundaries for security, privacy and individual control, and in encouraging interactions to take place. This will differ according to what those interactions can achieve. In some circumstances, maximising interaction will require government intervention to build the institutions and platforms that foster and sustain collaboration. And, sometimes, maximising interaction will involve creating institutions to develop the literacy and capabilities that individuals and organisations will need.

Left to their own devices, many of the dynamics of the Digital Revolution will exacerbate inequality in our society. Government interventions will be most beneficial if they are designed to be collaborative, not obstructive: if they enable everyone to be part of the opportunities created by these changes, rather than attempting to slow the effects of the Digital Revolution. Policies like the National Broadband Network, which was designed to ensure that the full opportunities of present and future technologies were extended to all Australians, are vital in this respect.

o

Australian governments at all levels should be looking at these changes and pursuing three kinds of policy intervention in order to realise the opportunities of the Digital Revolution for businesses, workers and consumers: building online communities, rolling back regulatory barriers and modernising our education system. Government is in a unique position to seed and sustain online communities. It can play a valuable role in providing the platforms, inter-operability standards, authentication services, privacy benchmarks and capacity building necessary to help bring these communities to critical mass. And it can encourage the 'emergent public goods' identified by Nicholas Gruen to flourish.

One area rich with possibilities is the creation of platforms that enable people to use real-time data about what others are doing to solve collective problems. Waze, a start-up acquired by Google in 2013, allows users to install an application on their smartphone that automatically shares the phone's location and movements with others, allowing an agglomeration of traffic congestion and flows to be passed on to users. Similarly, in Japan, Toyota's Big Data Traffic Information Service combines location and historical route data collected from its cars with other data collected from smartphones and infrastructure sensors. It provides real-time congestion data to both commuters and policy-makers.

The potential public benefits of these kinds of services are obvious, but it takes a lot of work for these communities to develop to the point where they're useful. Government is a unique facilitator of collective action. It could back a particular platform and use all arms of government to give it the best chance to work. It could contribute data to a chosen platform from its own car fleets, toll roads and public-transport systems. It could use the Department of Transport's website and social-media accounts to promote it, and even give tax breaks for early adopters (for example, through discounts on car registration or driver licences) if the platform creates spill-over benefits to the community.

At present, around four-fifths of Australians are walking around with a device in their pocket that has more processing power than the computers used for the moon landing, and GPS and accelerometer sensors that a decade ago were only available to the military. The potential to harness smartphones to solve collective problems is enormous, but little thought is devoted to it in policy circles today. If government did nothing else in this space but promoted communities where people could share information about the things they are doing that affect their fellow citizens, the public benefits would be enormous.

There are other contexts when it is more important for government to get out of the way. As a result of the Digital Revolution, it's now government intervention that represents a greater proportion of the total transaction costs facing business. Regulation can, and often does, deliver important public benefits. It can stop environmental harm or financial losses for consumers. But sometimes, especially during periods of rapid technological change, it prevents or hinders new, unanticipated things from emerging. This can be in the public interest, but it is more often in the private interests of specific groups with an unhealthy influence over policy-makers or regulators.

We might think it's a good thing that regulation requires taxi operators to obtain licences, undergo security checks and wear uniforms. But what if this regulation stops or hinders the emergence of new services that use a different method to provide a better customer experience? And what if an existing operator leverages their relationships with government and regulators to use regulation, rather than price and service, to compete with new providers?

Incumbents have a long history of resisting the introduction of new technologies. From the guild system in the seventeenth century effectively banning new methods of production to the Luddites in the nineteenth century destroying new machinery, beneficiaries of the status quo have often vigorously opposed technological change.

We're seeing a similar pattern in the twenty-first century. As disruptive innovators enter markets, they are met with litigation, calls for consumer boycotts, strikes, even violence, from incumbent businesses and workers. We've already seen robust regulatory stoushes over Uber's entry into the transport market, with the Victorian transport regulator pressing criminal charges against eleven Uber drivers in 2014. Similarly, Randwick Council in Sydney wrote to one Airbnb operator warning that she risked a million-dollar fine for running an 'unauthorised bed and breakfast'.

We need to develop institutional counterweights to those who seek to use regulation to hinder innovation. A dedicated commissioner within the Productivity Commission or the ACCC could spot circumstances where regulation is impeding digital innovations and act as a public-interest check on incumbents seeking regulations that will stop innovation. Giving the Office of Best Practice Regulation institutional freedom and independence with similar powers to the Parliamentary Budget Office might also be a worthy measure.

o

It's one thing for government to get out of the way of innovation; it's another to ensure that Australians have the literacy necessary to be innovators in a digital world. In his agenda-setting book *Average is Over*, Tyler Cowen explains how the best chess-playing entities in the world today are not human grandmasters or specialised super-computers, but rather 'freestyle' chess teams of people and computers. And the people on the best freestyle teams are not the smartest grandmasters but experts in collaboration. They're not teams of Magnus Carlsens and Garry Kasparovs; they're people with a deep understanding of the capabilities and limitations of computers.

The first winner of the Bank of Sweden's Prize in Economic Sciences in Memory of Alfred Nobel, Jan Tinbergen, argued that, since the introduction of factory automation, the jobs market in developed countries has been a race between education and technology. Where the pace of technological progress has outstripped the level of educational attainment in the workforce, wages have fallen relative to the amount of money made by the machines producing the goods. As a result of the Digital Revolution, technological progress has surged ahead in recent times. To keep up, Australian students and workers will need constantly to improve.

The skills required to enhance human productivity by using computers are different from those required either to perform the job well without a computer or to use existing computer programs to perform routine tasks. This means more than just being a competent user of existing devices or applications, a passive consumer of technology. People in the ICT sector describe it as being like the difference between knowing how to ride a tricycle and knowing how to ride a bicycle. Anyone can ride a tricycle within seconds of seeing one, but those who learn how to ride a bike can go to many more places.

Our schools are failing to teach these new, unique skills and ways of thinking that all workers will need in order to thrive in the Digital Revolution. This failure is most visible in the falling number of Australians studying the STEM subjects in high school: science, technology, engineering and mathematics.

Professor Ian Chubb, Australia's chief scientist, has said, 'As the economy becomes increasingly dependent on technology, our national competitiveness will be underwritten by our real-world capability in mathematics and science.' Workers in a wide range of professions outside the STEM disciplines now need to be able to evaluate and interpret statistical analysis and data modelling as part of their jobs. Despite this, fewer than one in ten Australian high-school students now complete the advanced-maths courses necessary to learn the basics of data analysis. The percentage of university students in maths degrees in Australia is only 0.5, roughly half the OECD average.

In Victoria, enrolments in the VCE ICT applications subject is at a twenty-year low, falling from fourteen thousand in 2000 to just 2,598 last year. Survey research undertaken by Microsoft suggests that around only a third of Australian students even have the opportunity of learning to code in school, either as a curriculum subject or as an extracurricular activity. The decline in the number of STEM students is flowing through to our universities in this area, too. The number of Australians enrolling in tertiary ICT courses fell by 52 per cent in the ten years between 2003 and 2013, from 8.1 per cent of all students to 3.9 per cent.

To date, Australia has sought to plug skills holes in the labour market through skilled migration and temporary migration. This might work for businesses seeking specific STEM skills in the short term, and it's certainly better than doing without, but it leaves Australian students and workers on the sidelines as the Digital Revolution sweeps across the globe.

○

Our education system will need to evolve to ensure that as many future workers as possible have the skills necessary to work with ever more complex machines, rather than competing against them. Countries like the United Kingdom and Estonia require all primary-school students to learn a problem-solving process called computational thinking, popularised by the computer scientist Jeannette Wing. It teaches students not a particular programming language but instead the conceptual 'power and limits of computing processes'. Computational thinking shows children how to frame problems so that they can be solved by computers, how to organise and analyse information, how to model and simulate data, and how to automate solutions using algorithms. Everyone would benefit from this understanding, even if they go on never to write a line of computer code in their lives.

In the absence of curriculum mandates, Australian philanthropic organisations using private funding, expertise and support have emerged that allow teachers to bring these skills into the classroom and students to hone them in their homes. Tim has sat in on a number of elective code clubs teaching the foundations of computational thinking at schools in Victoria. At Altona Primary, Eamon, a teacher with a passion for technology and the assistance of community grants from Mobil, moves around the classroom as kids sit on the floor with laptops and iPads solving robotics problems and coding video games. The code clubs are self-directed: kids learn in the classroom, then go home and teach themselves more via YouTube tutorials and by talking with each other. A series of these clubs is currently being supported across Australia by the Telstra Foundation.

Government could collaborate with these industry and philanthropically led initiatives, and provide funding to allow disadvantaged schools to acquire the hardware and software necessary to participate in them. An online support network for ICT teachers could be established to bring it all together, offering teaching resources and support materials and a place for teachers and students to share their findings. Local government could then partner with the private sector to create an extracurricular infrastructure for enthusiastic students to develop their own skills beyond those of their peers. They could encourage such study by creating interschool competition and national prizes in game design and robotics.

Government could also support the teaching of data analysis in the classroom by making its data sets available for students to use. We could set up analysis challenges that allow schools to compete through team-based problem-solving to come up with the best analysis. What if a school science competition went further than a display at the local university: what if it went to solving parking problems in the local shopping centre instead? We'll only increase the number of Australian students studying STEM subjects by solving the demand problem, and to do so we've got to make kids *want* to study it. We're most likely to be able to achieve this if we can teach it in ways that are relevant to their lives.

Women's participation in STEM learning and employment is an important equity issue in the Digital Revolution. Half as many girls take advanced-maths classes in high school as boys do. Girls make up just 16 per cent of ICT applications students, 6 per cent of software-development students and 2 per cent of systems-engineering students. In higher education, women account for 44 per cent of STEM students, though they make up 56 per cent of students overall. Once health sciences and nursing are taken out of the picture, the imbalance is extreme. In ICT areas, 15 per cent of students in higher education in

2010 were women; in engineering, 14 per cent. As the importance of STEM skills across all professions increases, the costs to women will rise. Instead of the wage gap closing, it will widen.

It's unsurprising that less than one in five of Australia's 229,000 ICT professionals are women. A 2015 report by the Department of Employment projects that the number of professionals will grow to over 266,000 by 2019. To achieve gender parity by this time, we'll need almost 100,000 more female ICT professionals than we have today. It's no small task.

Some American universities have been able to increase the proportion of women enrolling in, and completing, their computer-science classes by offering pre-tutorials covering the basics of the subject. These courses address the reality that many men have been able to pick up the skills before attending university because society constantly exposes them to, and encourages them to experiment with, computers. We believe that code clubs targeted at girls in primary school and other gender-based early intervention STEM classes may be able to increase rates of female participation. If we can instill in girls an early sense of digital capability, it would encourage them to pursue further study. Other approaches might also be needed—but this is a critical start.

○

The Digital Revolution won't just reshape our economy. It has the potential to transform the way our government works. Ric Simes, a former economic adviser to Paul Keating and partner at Deloitte, has argued that over the next twenty years policy-makers should develop a coherent strategy for promoting technological innovation in government services like health, education and transport. In competition-exposed segments of our economy, market forces are already prodding private providers to innovate as they compete for customers, leading to greater choice and convenience. We've seen much slower progress in the public sector.

The emergence of online communities presents an opportunity for government to radically improve its responsiveness and efficiency where market forces like price signals are not possible or appropriate. As Friedrich Hayek saw last century, a market is at its core an information-aggregation system. It aggregates all available information about consumer demand in the form of a price. Under the right conditions, the American author and scholar Cass Sunstein has noted, online communities of interest offer an alternative way to aggregate and share information sourced from around the globe.

The Digital Revolution has allowed specialised communities of interest to form that are dedicated even to the most obscure subjects in our society, producing unprecedented volumes of specific and constantly evolving expertise and commentary. But these communities have many shortcomings compared to markets. Chief among these is that they don't have the same carrots and sticks attached to the information they aggregate. For institutions where price signals cannot or should not be used, though, they offer the possibility of significant information gains.

Today, three in four Australians prefer to interact with government online or on the phone, rather than in person. People who interact with government online often have strong interests and expertise in the subject matter of the online platform that they are using. A fisherman applying for a fishing licence from the government may rely on this interaction for his livelihood. Over time, a person applying for large numbers of these licences may develop unique insights into the effectiveness of the licensing system, and into what best meets the needs of fishermen while still protecting our maritime environment. But at present this kind of expertise is left latent and wasted. The users of government services have no way to efficiently share their knowledge, either with the providers of these services or with other users of them.

Online communities could allow members to learn from each other's experiences, reducing the costs of administration for government. They could also allow government to learn from participants' experiences, offering a low-cost way of identifying areas of under-performance or unmet need. Private businesses already encourage the emergence of online communities as a source of innovation and to support their products and services. The American ICT research firm Gartner has estimated that organisations which integrate online communities into customer support can reduce their costs by up to half.

There's no reason that online communities couldn't deliver similar outcomes for citizens and government. The customer-service challenges facing Centrelink and Medicare have a lot in common with the challenges facing large banks and telecommunications companies. They're all large organisations that manage hundreds of often complex services and millions of interactions a day, directly with people.

o

We need to reconceptualise government: to stop thinking of it as a top-down provider of services, and to start constructing open architectures for people to participate in the delivery of government services. Making online communities work will require different things from government in different circumstances. Sometimes government will need to help with building scale within the communities, or with moderation as these communities grow. Sometimes its task will be the verification of identities and information, and sometimes it will be certifying what is being produced at the end for other users. All of this will require new skills and a new way of thinking about the nature of government. It's not the difference between big government and small government; it's the difference between closed government and open government, finding more effective ways of providing the fundamental services that governments should provide.

We can start by looking at government as a facilitator of communities. Take health care. People living with serious and chronic diseases often seek out others with similar conditions for support and to share information about how they cope with their daily challenges. A shared illness is a strong common interest: in the most serious cases, strong enough for people to bear the costs in time and money of real-world support groups. What if government created a platform where people could start their own support groups—sites where patients are given the tools to track their own health indicators and compare them not only to a demographically similar baseline, but to individuals with the same condition with whom they could interact online? What if GPs didn't just give patients referrals to medical specialists, but also to social networks of people living with similar conditions? And what if government provided ongoing medical support to these networks by paying specialist nurses with online community-management skills to participate in the communities?

There are already private-sector models for how this could work. PatientsLikeMe, an online American network, allows people to connect with others who have the same medical conditions, to track and share their own experiences. It currently has more than 300,000 members and offers support networks for more than 2,300 conditions, including Parkinson's disease, HIV/AIDS, MS and mood conditions. It allows people to integrate data tracked by pedometers and health monitors on smartphones. It's not perfect, but it's slick and easy to use, looking more like a social-media platform. And it's barely scratching the surface of the potential for online communities to support the health and general well-being of patients.

○

Innovation is notoriously hard for government. Ministers and bureaucrats don't have the same market incentives as the private sector does, the constant fear of economic loss that pushes them to try new ways of doing things. Bureaucracy is more risk averse and costs are more constrained in the public sector. Online communities are a way to harness the experience and expertise of creative minds outside government to reinvigorate public-sector innovation.

One way that this can happen is through challenge platforms: online competitions that allow public entities to challenge users and innovators outside their organisation to solve their problems, offering prizes for solutions. The best challenge platforms also allow communities of innovators and users to form around the platform, pooling skills and directing their talents towards specific problems.

The Challenge.gov platform has involved more than 150,000 innovators in solving more than four hundred technical, scientific and creative challenges posed by American government departments and agencies. The site is currently hosting challenges from groups as diverse as the Environmental Protection Agency, the Consumer Product Safety Commission, NASA, and the Department of Housing and Urban Development. One challenge, from the National Sciences Foundation, offers a million-dollar prize for creating a product to 'increase the speed and accuracy of digitisation of a drawer of insect specimens and their associated data'—the information written on labels attached to pins in display cases. Challenge.gov has also solved bigger problems. A challenge to build a car with a fuel economy of one hundred miles per gallon that was capable of mass production, partly funded by the Department of Energy, netted the three winners US$10 million in prize money and private investment equivalent to US$100 million.

The Australian government should establish a national challenge platform of its own as soon as possible. To kick-start things, government could also establish an innovation fund that would allocate funding to be used as prizes on the platform, in response to pitches from departments and agencies about the problems facing their operations and the expected returns on solving them. The Department of Transport could make a bid for a commuting smartphone application and platform that reduced congestion in a particular area by a specified amount with a reward commensurate to the target's value to the community. The Department of Health could make a bid for the development of a wearable device that increased physical activity within a target community by a defined level with a reward that reflected the health costs of unchecked obesity in the community. The fund could act like an in-house venture-capital arm for government, spurring enterprise in the public sector.

○

Digital data is the fuel of the Digital Revolution. And collectively we've barely begun to explore the uses that we can put it to. Right now, most of the data being created around the world is private, proprietary data. It's sitting in servers somewhere, owned by individual companies and used exclusively by their staff, contractors and clients.

When data is open—legally and practically able to be accessed and reused by others—it has a different and greater value. Data that is available, timely, in bulk sets, machine-readable and openly licensed is, for all intents and purposes, a public good. Like lighthouses and clean air, its use by one person doesn't limit its capacity to be used by anyone else.

In the public sector, open data enables accountability and transparency, and informs policy analysis and decision-making, innovation and service delivery. It can make service delivery more efficient and policy decision-making more effective by helping government to make better, data-based predictions. In New Zealand, for example, the Ministry of Social Development is using data analytics to target mentoring and education towards individuals at a high risk of welfare dependency. Open data can also highlight the relationships between issues being confronted by government, creating opportunities for prioritising expenditure. Analysis of open data in the United States showed one local government how public complaints about delays in garbage collection in particular areas preceded expensive rat infestations soon after.

In the private sector, open data informs decision-making and innovation, and allows for the creation of entirely new products and services. Queensland Globe is an open-data product that makes spatial data collected by the state government available as overlays on Google Earth. This includes addresses and property boundaries, public infrastructure, land parcels and tenure, flood and topographical maps. It has become a crucial resource for farmers, engineers, lawyers, town planners and property investors.

Open data isn't just a technology issue. It's a mainstream policy issue for every developed economy. The McKinsey Global Institute has identified substantial benefits from the use of open data in education, transport, consumer products, electricity, oil and gas, health care and consumer finance, and estimates that its total value worldwide is US$3.2 trillion.

However, as with other public goods, there's a collective-action problem that limits our realising the full benefits of data. As individuals do not pay directly to access open data, less of it is produced than would be reflected by its total value to society. As with other public goods, this is where government should come in. A comprehensive national policy to create a consistent framework for the collection, storage, use and transformation of open data within business, the government and community would greatly increase the volume and utility of the open data collected in Australia. Just as government invested in lighthouses in the nineteenth century, so too must it invest in a framework to facilitate the use of open data for the twenty-first century.

○

There are a number of ways in which the federal government can intervene to help create more open data in Australia. At the most basic level, it should open up existing government data sets. Geospatial data, environmental data, statistical data, public registers, government-property inventories, land-use data: all of this is collected by government as a matter of course, but is also of enormous value to people in the community and to business. Thanks to the hard work of many individuals, Australia has made more progress on this front than most other countries.

Government should also be collecting more data and building platforms to make this data available to the public. In an age of cheap telemetry, there is much more about our world that we could be measuring. The Singapore government is planning a Smart Nation Platform to connect 'everyone to everything, everywhere, all the time' in the island state. It intends to use sensors to collect information, then use co-ordinated data sharing and analysis to comprehend it, and to make this information and analysis available to citizens, policy-makers and business. The potential is enormous. We currently spend almost twenty billion dollars on road construction and maintenance in Australia every year. An insight that improved the efficiency of this spending by only a fraction of a per cent would quickly add up to a very large saving to the nation.

Another way that we can increase the value of open data is to collect and make available more real-time information. At present, government and policy-makers rely heavily on data that shows snapshots of our environment and our economy at a moment in the past. But we now have the tools to collect, aggregate and make available large amounts of data in real-time: what American economists have called nowcasting. (This can include credit-card, package-delivery, financial, public-transport patronage and fare, and toll-road patronage and fare data.) It could provide insights into the immediate state of our economy and community, and help improve decisions on monetary and fiscal policy.

Just as the fisherman cares more about his fishing licence than does the bureaucrat behind the desk, so the community activist cares more about the truck fumes affecting her children than does the department collecting the data. Government could allow engaged citizens like these to collect and contribute data to public platforms in a way that could allow it to be monitored and analysed alongside government data. Tasmania's Sense-T project integrates data from public and private environmental and agricultural sensors around Tasmania on a platform that allows it to be reused and transformed for use in mobile applications and other online services. This community-collected data has proved to be of significant value to the local viticulture, aquaculture and agriculture industries. The US Environmental Protection Agency has created an online platform that allows members of the public to install sensors in their communities and to contribute environmental data about their neighbourhood to inform the regulator's enforcement action. We should create similar mechanisms for the collection and sharing of community data in our own neighbourhoods.

Finally, government should establish frameworks that allow citizens to make an informed decision about sharing the personal data they create through interactions with both the public and private sectors with other parties. This will both create new sources of usable data and increase the public's confidence that they have control over the way their data is used. Personal Information Management Services (PIMS) enable individuals to control the collection and use of their personal information by both government and private organisations. They require data collectors to provide each individual with access to their data in a portable, open format that can be used by third parties if the person allows it. These third parties could solicit individuals' information in exchange for the provision of other services. And individuals could donate their data to researchers trying to solve important public-interest problems.

Australia ought to take steps towards universal PIMS as soon as possible. We could start by establishing a voluntary system based on the English midata program and mandating the participation of a range of government service providers.

A more ambitious government could develop a policy for public–private partnerships to actively collect *private* data of strategic importance. Nicholas Gruen believes that the federal government should pursue this in order to compile the world's largest database for human genes. He points out that private-sector DNA-profiling companies like 23andMe can replicate 180 genetic associations with documented medical conditions for a hundred dollars per person.

In Australia, Sydney's Garvan Institute of Medical Research is one of a handful of facilities in the world that have the infrastructure to sequence an entire human genome for under a thousand dollars: information that could assist in the diagnosis of an extraordinary range of diseases. The data collected through this testing is valuable to individuals, as it can give them a better understanding of their genetic vulnerabilities and prompt them to take preventative health steps in response. It is valuable to the government, as it would reduce the costs of screening and diagnostic testing, allow for better targeted health-care interventions, and alert health-care providers to potentially costly allergies and drug incompatibilities. Finally, the data could be a boon for Australian medical researchers, particularly if it could be coupled with other data sources associated with the individual and provided through PIMS. Australia could quickly become a global hub for medical research and treatment.

Gruen argues that, because of the broad public benefits, it would make sense to nudge individuals to undergo this testing by bulk billing the service. The mass collection of genomic profiles poses tricky privacy and ethical challenges, and is easier for an economist than a politician to propose, but it's an example of the kind of big-picture initiatives with large payoffs that will be possible if we start laying the groundwork now.

Increasing the availability of open data is only half the equation. Governments need to learn how to integrate data collection and analysis to their policy-making processes. To do this, we should invest in the creation of an Australian centre of excellence for data analysis, a National Data Analytics Centre (NDAC). It would be a long-term, strategic investment in our national capability to use this new resource of the digital age.

The NDAC could be responsible for creating a public clearing house to aggregate all the streams of data being produced by government, community and the private sector. It could then become a central source of data-analysis expertise for the federal government, providing expert support to its departments and agencies. It could model best practice, and teach good data collection, aggregation and analysis to Australian policy-makers and public servants, academics and think-tanks. And it could also assist government to test policy effectiveness by helping policy-makers to set up randomised policy trials on the digital plane.

The NDAC could bring together data scientists and experts from state and federal governments, the Australian Bureau of Statistics, the private sector, academia, and regulators like the Privacy Commissioner and the Information Commissioner. It would be a national figurehead of data-analysis skills, and it would help to equip all Australians with the skills to receive the benefits that open data can offer.

○

One way or another, our daily lives will be different in twenty-five years' time as a result of the Digital Revolution. The pace of change, and that the change is being driven by technical innovations which most people don't fully understand, can feel scary. In this, at least, there's nothing new. As Genevieve Bell, the Australian in-house anthropologist at Intel, has identified, technological innovations that threaten to change our relationships to time, space and other people have always engendered community panic about the effect on society. Railways, electricity, television, the internet, mobile phones and social media: all led to calls for government to do something about the threat they supposedly posed.

Over time these public anxieties dissipate, but the way government responds to technological innovation still matters. Flip responses can blind us to the opportunities afforded by innovations. On the other hand, it can be just as damaging for government to be paralysed in the face of technological change. If we take control of our future and shape the changes to our society, that future will be unimaginably better and not just unrecognisable.

4

Climate

AT FIRST BLUSH, the little town of Old Bar doesn't look like the frontline of climate change in Australia. On any given day, kids play in cul de sacs, dogs yap in front yards and surfers paddle out beyond the breaks. But the For Sale signs on the footpaths in front of beach-front properties tell a different story.

Old Bar is the most rapidly eroding part of the New South Wales coastline. Since the early 2000s, a metre of beachfront has been lost each year. In 2012, it was reported that the local surf club may not see out the decade and the primary school is at risk. In parts of town, homes cannot be insured against erosion and properties once valued at millions of dollars are now worthless. In June 2014, the local council approved plans to protect Old Bar by building an anti-erosion wall along two kilometres of coastline. But the council cannot afford to pay for it. The state government has refused to fund the wall, fearing it will set a precedent. The people of Old Bar, it seems, are on their own.

Old Bar's problems are not all caused by climate change, but the town is neveretheless a sign of things to come. Erosion and rising seas are problems on their own, but bigger ones when wild weather hits. A one-metre rise in the shoreline can easily translate into four metres during a storm surge.

The issue of how we manage a changing climate in Australia is no longer theoretical. Whatever action we take to try to slow or stop global warming, some warming has already occurred and more has been locked in to 2040. Life is going to change in Australia's cities, on its coasts and in the bush. Yet basic questions about how we will adapt to hotter, more volatile conditions have barely registered in the national psyche.

To date, carbon pricing as a means of limiting climate change has been the focus of Australia's stunted global-warming debate. Carbon pricing is critical, because the world is on a trajectory to a level of global warming that humans will find it very difficult to adapt to. In the national debate, climate has been pitted against the economy in a political game and the public have been asked to choose a winner. But not acting on climate change is already costing us. A clean-energy revolution, with plenty of positive spill-overs, is already underway. Our big competitors are getting on the path to lower-pollution economies, leaving us behind. We are uniquely placed to grasp the economic opportunities presented by climate change, but if we do not act soon they will pass us by.

The path forward is clear. We need to take action to mitigate climate change. And we'll reap big rewards if we do it quickly. We need to plan now for substantial adaptation in our cities, in regional areas and on our coasts. Currently, we're not doing these things in any serious way. What's holding us back is the toxic, negative and depressing tone of Australian climate politics. To get the policy right, this is going to have to change.

But whatever we choose to do on a political or policy front, one thing is certain: in the decades to 2040, we're going to be hearing a lot more stories like that of Old Bar.

○

The science of climate change leads us to three main policy conclusions. First, by 2050, the world must dramatically decrease pollution (our shorthand for greenhouse gases). Second, to avoid a costly and dislocating adjustment, we should start transitioning to a low-pollution economy as soon as possible. Third, even with dramatic action, some global warming is unavoidable. Australia must prepare to adapt.

Humans are the main contributors to the global warming that has occurred in recent decades, because we create pollution. Scientists are as confident that pollution is causing global warming as they are that smoking causes lung cancer. In Australia, the major contributors are electricity generation (especially coal), agriculture (mostly cattle and fertiliser), transport, industrial processes (such as aluminium and cement manufacturing) and the destruction of forests.

Globally, pollution is being pumped into the atmosphere faster than it is being broken down by plants. The oceans are absorbing pollution, endangering the marine environment. Pollution is building up, like a bathtub with a small plughole and the tap left on full. Its concentration in the atmosphere has risen from approximately 285 parts per million of carbon-dioxide equivalent in the mid-1800s to around 445 today. This accumulated pollution acts like a blanket: the sun's energy is trapped in the atmosphere after it bounces off the Earth's surface.

We often hear commentators say that no single severe-weather event—storm or bushfire, drought or flood—can be attributed to climate change. Technically, this is true. We cannot be certain whether a natural disaster would have happened anyway. But we can be certain that climate change loads the dice towards more extreme-weather events, just as smoking loads the dice towards lung cancer.

As with smoking and lung cancer, there is a delay between pollution entering the atmosphere and the globe warming. This is a fundamental principle of climate science. Pollution we emit today will affect the Earth's temperature many years into the future. The world is already 0.8 degrees Celsius hotter today than it was one hundred and fifty years ago—which accords with predictions that eminent climate scientists made twenty years ago.

The Intergovernmental Panel on Climate Change (IPCC), the global authority on climate change, predicts that by 2040 the temperature will probably be between 1.6 and 2 degrees warmer than it was before industrialisation. By 2100, the range explodes: we may well face temperature increases from 1.6 to 4.9 degrees. The policies we put in place today will help to determine at which end of this spectrum we will sit.

Australia has a great deal to lose from a changing climate. As a nation we struggle to cope even with the temperature change we've experienced so far. The summer of 2013—the Angry Summer—changed many Australians' perceptions of life in the sunburnt country. The Angry Summer was the country's hottest since records began: some 123 temperature records were broken. Devastating bushfires burned across the country. Heatwaves do not provide the same dramatic footage, but they ravaged cities and towns. As the month drew to a close, New South Wales and Queensland were hit by severe flooding. When the Angry Summer was over, millions had been affected, thousands had had property destroyed, and hundreds had died or been injured.

Because Australia is already exposed to climate extremes, any increase in temperature is likely to have severe effects. In the city, the number of heat-related deaths, particularly among the elderly and homeless, will rise. Australian homes have always been destroyed in bushfires; with climate change, this will likely happen more often. Sea levels will rise, both from melting glaciers and ice sheets, and because warmer water takes up more space. State, federal and household budgets will be under pressure due to the costs associated with increased flooding, and the strain on roads, rail lines and public buildings will intensify. Beyond damage to assets, agricultural yields will likely decline and some natural wonders, like the Great Barrier Reef, will likely deteriorate.

Climate change is expected to increase the number of displaced persons in our region. Cyclone Pam left half the Vanuatu population homeless, and sea-level rises are destroying crops on several low-lying islands. This will become more common between now and 2040. The Australian and New Zealand governments have already received immigration applications from Pacific Islanders identifying as climate-change refugees.

All of these changes will occur with an average temperature increase of 2 degrees Celsius. Under the IPCC's worst-case scenario, the world will reach an average increase of 4 degrees around the 2080s. Climate-change impacts are non-linear: the impact of 4 degrees of warming is likely to be much worse than twice as bad as 2 degrees of warming. With 4 degrees of warming, Australia is likely to experience heavy loss of life due to increased heatwaves. The number of extreme-fire-danger days will rise by 100 to 300 per cent. With a 0.5 metre sea-level rise (the IPCC's midpoint prediction for 2100), the Climate Commission predicted that coastal flooding which would usually have happened once a century will occur ten times a year. CSIRO modelling suggests that, at 4 degrees of warming, the rich tropical rainforest of the Cairns region could look like Jabiru in the Northern Territory—one of the hottest, driest parts of the continent. Imagine an Australia where outdoor summer tennis is a distant memory, we can spend no longer than thirty minutes at the beach before getting badly burnt and the bushfire season runs from September to April.

Globally, beyond 2040, Professor Ross Garnaut and other researchers have forecast shocking regional instability if climate change is left unchecked. In a 4-degree-warmer world, according to their estimates, 250 million people will be seeking resettlement in the Asia-Pacific alone. It's not the smaller Pacific islands that will produce these vast numbers. Bangladesh and low-lying coastal towns in China, Indonesia and India pose the most substantial resettlement challenges. Due to our proximity to these countries and our low population density, Australia will be under pressure to take its fair share. Other problems that will affect the stability of our region, such as poverty, conflict and access to energy, will be also exacerbated by a changing climate.

Today, we are on track to exceed 4 degrees of warming over the next century. In these conditions, our grandchildren and great-grandchildren may face increased infectious diseases, water scarcity and conflict. This is not to mention the impact of natural disasters that will result in more deaths, and threaten livelihoods. To shift back to 2 degrees of warming, scientists argue that the world needs roughly to halve overall carbon emissions by 2050 and reach zero net emissions in the second half of this century. The further we are from these targets, the greater the risk we will face.

The window to limit global temperature increases to 2 degrees may still be open. But not for long.

○

For many years now, powerful figures in Australia have argued that it is too costly to take real action on climate change. And a broad community of progressives—policy-makers, politicians and activists—have claimed that beyond these short-term costs lies a wealth of opportunity; that Australia can thrive in a low-carbon economy and it is in our interests to be an early mover.

Today, several things have become clear. Carbon pricing works. The costs of failing to act, and the benefits of doing so, are becoming apparent. Claims of green growth and jobs, once derided as fantasy, are fast becoming reality.

Renewable-energy technologies, which will allow economies to continue to grow while reducing pollution, have progressed much faster than was expected. While renewable energy can be expensive to build, the process of generating energy through some renewables is already much cheaper than fossil fuels. In the case of wind turbines, they are less expensive to build than a coal plant and much less expensive to operate.

Moore's Law (named after Gordon Moore of Intel) stated that the number of transistors per square inch on integrated circuits would double each year. Now we have Swanson's Law (named after Richard Swanson, an American solar-energy guru), which predicts that the cost of producing solar panels will fall by 20 per cent for each doubling of production. Recent data suggests that we are out-performing Swanson's prediction. In 1977 the cost per watt of electricity generated by solar was US$77, and in 2014 the cost had plummeted to less than seventy cents. Over the last five years alone, the cost of solar generation has halved.

Even accounting for these advances, the space for innovation and invention in renewable energy remains massive. Professor Martin Green, a solar researcher at the University of New South Wales, has said that 'it's horse and buggy days as far as solar is concerned at the moment.' Last year, Green and his colleagues broke the world record for solar-energy conversion. Elsewhere, nanomaterials a fraction of the width of a human hair are being used to improve solar efficiency. Researchers at the University of Melbourne are experimenting with plastic solar cells that can be printed directly onto roof tiles.

The next challenge for scientists and innovators is energy storage. Renewable-energy generation is intermittent. Solar, for example, creates energy while the sun is out, but to replace fossil fuels, we need to store energy for use whenever it is needed. Earlier this year, the electric-car company Tesla released a concept battery that will allow households and small commercial premises to store solar power during the day for use at night. Battery storage is a game changer. UBS, the global investment bank, has predicted that big fossil-fuel companies may provide little more than back-up power within ten to twenty years.

Another technology tackling the storage problem is pumped storage, where water is pumped up to a higher point using solar or wind power, then released to generate hydro power when required. Australia has two large hydro-power schemes, the Snowy Mountains in New South Wales and Hydro Tasmania. If pumped-storage technology takes off, there will be scope for these two stations to provide more renewable energy in Australia's southern states.

Hydrogen is another storage method at advanced stages in Japan, Germany and France. An electric current is passed through water when there is surplus renewable-energy production. This current releases hydrogen and oxygen. The hydrogen is then captured and used later. In Japan, it is already possible to go into a Toyota dealer and buy a hydrogen-powered car.

Beyond renewable energy, more commercial buildings are receiving energy-efficient retrofits. In our homes, we are about to go well beyond energy-efficient light bulbs. Digitised appliances will automatically adjust energy use based on household schedules, and washing machines and hot-water systems will operate automatically when electricity prices are low.

These are just some of the technologies in the works today. Where things might go next is difficult to predict. Australia could be a central part of this world of innovation. But the countries that will lead, and benefit most, are those that move fast.

Lord Nicholas Stern and other leading economists have talked of 'a new energy-industrial revolution, involving a wave of innovation, discovery, creativity and investment', noting how historically similar revolutions have spawned decades of prosperity. Supporting Stern's conclusions, research by Cambridge Econometrics finds that reducing carbon emissions in Britain to around 60 per cent below 1990 levels by 2030 would increase economic growth by over 1 per cent in net terms, leading to additional jobs and income for households.

In Australia's case, we're better positioned to benefit than most developed economies. Australia has natural advantages in renewable energy—wind and water, open space and sunlight. Because Australia has strong institutional structures and capable governments, the nation is well placed to plan for the complex adjustments ahead. We have a highly skilled workforce and a history of innovation in clean energy. Scientists at the CSIRO produced the UltraBattery, which improved the viability of hybrid and electric vehicles all over the world. Other renewable-energy technologies coming from the CSIRO include air-turbine systems, solar-thermal air conditioning and the use of geothermal heat energy for desalination.

Despite these advances, opportunities to capture the benefits of renewable-energy innovations are slipping through Australia's grasp. The part of Australia that gets the least light, the southwest coast of Tasmania, sees about the same amount of sunshine as Germany's sunniest point. But, today, Germany is among the global leaders in renewable energy. In 2011, the country adopted the *Energiewende* (energy transformation), an aggressive new energy policy. Renewable-energy companies have flocked to Germany, almost four hundred thousand jobs have been created and renewables now supply almost 30 per cent of the nation's energy needs.

Meanwhile, Australia is moving backwards. In 2014, international investment in renewable energy soared 16 per cent, to a new record of US$310 billion. Locally, a divisive political struggle over the Renewable Energy Target saw investment in Australian renewables plummet by 90 per cent. Over roughly the same period, a million renewable-energy jobs were created globally, but in Australia more than two thousand were lost. Some green-energy producers and financiers reconsidered their local options, some shifted investment to other countries, some left altogether. All cited an unstable, uncertain policy framework.

One companies shift their focus elsewhere, it's hard to get them back. Jobs, taxes and the commercial benefits of innovation are lost overseas. Firms in innovative industries tend to cluster together (like tech companies do in Silicon Valley) because there are benefits in locating near one another. Proximity encourages interactions between business, research institutions and government that, in turn, generate ideas. Green technologies are especially likely to benefit from clustering. Relative to older fossil-fuel-based patents, green patents in the energy and transport sectors are over 40 per cent more likely to be used in other inventions. For instance, battery-storage technology can be used in electric cars, and also to power businesses and homes. Once established, clusters tend to become self-fulfilling, as the scientists, inventors, innovators and entrepreneurs who want to be where the action is move to global centres for innovation.

Australia needs more success stories like First Solar, which is investing hundreds of millions of dollars in plants throughout regional New South Wales and creating more than six hundred jobs. But we need to support these companies with the right policy mix. Carbon pricing, compensatory cash transfers, targets for renewable-energy electricity supply, energy research and development, and government-backed finance for commercialisation of early stage renewable-energy technologies will be part of the solution.

The right policies will help Australia capitalise on our natural advantages while managing the short-term costs of transition. Today, we are at grave risk of missing out as other countries beat us to the punch. And the longer we delay action on climate, the more long-life emissions-intensive investments—like fossil fuel plants, energy-intensive buildings, and road instead of rail—are made that lock us in to a high-pollution economy. The more dependent on pollution our economy becomes, the more it will ultimately cost to shift to a low-pollution approach.

○

There will be short-term costs in making the transition to a low-carbon economy. While non-energy-intensive sectors will likely expand—such as renewable energy, gas extraction, lithium and light rail—transitioning to a low-pollution economy will have significant ramifications for Australia's energy-intensive sectors, such as coal, aluminium, beef and road transport.

In making the transition required, here, too, Australia is better positioned than most nations to adjust. ClimateWorks, an Australian climate-change think-tank, is part of a global project underway in fifteen high-pollution countries. The organisation has worked with academics and scientists to map a path for Australia to reach a zero-pollution economy by 2050. Across the different countries, the basic mechanisms are the same: we need to improve energy efficiency and switch to renewables. But in doing so, Australia has options that aren't available elsewhere. Abundant solar and wind resources will help, and so too will the fact that Australia has by far the highest area of arable land, per capita, of all countries. This additional resource will allow Australia to offset some pollution by planting trees to absorb pollution that is prohibitively expensive to avoid.

There's a popular argument that Australia constitutes a relatively small share of global pollution, so mitigation efforts are largely beyond its control. Certainly, Australia's pollution is not on the same scale as in China, India or the United States. However, we account for 1.3 per cent of all pollution—making us the thirteenth-largest emitter in the world and the highest per capita among OECD countries. If we include Australia's coal exports, this substantially increases Australia's global contribution.

When acting on climate change is seen as a medium-term opportunity, the argument that Australia accounts for only a small share of total emissions is largely irrelevant. Climate action is a race toward economic transition, and Australia is mixing in the back half of developed countries. In November 2014, the Climate Council reported that thirty-nine countries and twenty sub-national jurisdictions are putting a price on carbon. Following its publication, and just prior to the G20 leaders' meeting in Brisbane, China and the United States announced an agreement to reduce their nations' pollution. On home soil, Australia was exposed as a straggler. Our national debate is still focused on how to cut emissions by 5 per cent by 2020. In the meantime, the global policy community has moved on to the quest to reach zero emissions in the second half of the century.

Aggressive global targets are in Australia's interests, because we are uniquely positioned both to grow in a low-pollution world and to mitigate pollution in our domestic economy. And taking action in Australia can stimulate mitigation progress in other countries. We can do so by demonstration—by proving that good policy can reduce pollution and bring climate change under control. And by diplomacy—by using our sway in the international community to advocate for change. But we will have little influence on the global discussion until we have acted on climate ourselves.

○

In 2010, Brown Brothers winemakers, whose long-time home is in northeast Victoria, purchased a vineyard near Launceston, in Tasmania's north. Brown Brothers made the decision in part to position their business for Australia's changing climate. Tasmania has a small but proud tradition of producing cool-climate wines and, as the weather warms, the island state's wine industry is projected to grow. Meanwhile, a study by the National Academy of Sciences recently found that more than 70 per cent of Australian land currently used for growing wine grapes could become unsuitable for this purpose by 2050.

Whatever we do to mitigate climate change, Australia is adapting—and will need to keep adapting—to warmer, more volatile conditions. And, unlike for Brown Brothers, there won't always be a neat solution. The adaptation task is vast, almost unquantifiable. But the quicker we confront it, the better we are going to be able to manage.

To 2040, coastal areas will need to protect themselves against erosion by preserving natural environmental features, such as mangroves and sand dunes, and preventing development where flooding risk will be too great. In cities, we need to determine how we will bring down the temperature in built-up areas—for example, by setting aside land for public parks and planting additional trees—and think through how best to protect vulnerable residents. In regional centres, farmers will need carefully to select crops that will thrive in different conditions, and develop long-term water-security plans. All these things will take time.

At the core of successful adaptation is resilience, and this requires that two challenges be met by the Australian community today. We need to understand what is coming, sooner rather than later, so we have the time and flexibility to prepare and respond. And we need to figure out who is responsible for adaptation, and who will pay the costs.

Building resilience in our natural environment will help us cope with a changing climate. If the environment is weak, it will deteriorate in the face of even small temperature changes. The Great Barrier Reef is under a great deal of environmental stress—from ocean acidification, salinity, dredging and predators such as the crown-of-thorns starfish. All these add to the fragility of the reef, making it more susceptible to degradation due to a warming climate. To preserve the future livelihood of many coastal Queensland towns and cities, it's essential to reduce these pressures.

The same applies to Australia's forest systems. As the temperature changes, some species are seeking cooler climes: moving south or to higher elevation. Many forest-dwelling animals, once they reach the end of the forest system, find further migration is difficult. We need to ensure where possible that fauna have the opportunity to adapt—for example, by protecting parks and open space between forests, which today allow animals safely to migrate from one environment to another.

Resilience will help us manage international as well as domestic challenges. Australia is in a position to help people in our region develop skills and tools to assist them to adapt to climate change. Kiribati, the small island nation in the Pacific, faces the prospect of being swallowed up by the rising ocean. Through its aid program, the Australian government is providing nursing training to more than eighty Kiribati citizens. If they are forced to migrate to another country, they will do so with skills that will be needed where they end up, affording them a better chance of choosing their destination and a means of employment when they get to their new home.

To plan for the future, good information is essential. Some local councils have recognised this: in 2011 the City of Greater Geelong released its climate-change adaptation strategy, which outlined local climate risks, priority adaptation actions and how adaptation decisions would be made. Ideas outlined in our Technology chapter will be relevant, including harnessing the innovative potential of online communities, and more strategic collection and use of data. A publicly run website is an obvious portal through which to distribute information on local climate risks. Australians could enter their address and receive a range of tailored climate-change information, including bushfire and flood mapping. Climate Kelpie, early out of the blocks, already provides resources for farmers across the country. Users can look up medium- to long-range weather forecasts, download modelling tools, and contact other farmers in their industry who are living in their region and managing the same climate risks.

The new website could expand on Climate Kelpie by including up-to-date area-hazard maps, disaster-mitigation initiatives and plans for specific vulnerabilities. Where heatwaves are a risk, there could be listings for places that will always be kept cool and accessible. (The Coastal Climate Blueprint and the NARCliM websites are steps in the right direction.)

While governments can provide information to help Australians adapt to a changing climate, they cannot bear all the costs of adaptation. Over time, the bill will be prohibitive. And when costs are not planned for, those least able to afford to adapt are going to be left in the most precarious position.

Insurance markets will be a powerful tool to assist Australian businesses, families and communities in adapting to climate-change risks. Pooling risk across communities so that no one community is bankrupted by a severe climactic event is a valuable service. More subtly, differences in insurance prices deter future development in areas at high risk of bushfires, flooding or erosion.

However, insurance coverage is not equally distributed within communities. Those on lower incomes tend to underinvest in insurance policies. People with fewer resources tend to have difficulty estimating the value of their assets. They also lack trusted advice and accessible information to compare insurance products, and many have had negative experiences with insurance companies. To ensure that the most vulnerable aren't the least protected, government may need to play a role in providing means-tested insurance subsidies for households in high-risk areas. It's imperative that we remove state-based insurance taxes.

Insurance counselling can also foster more equal coverage. A government website that provides price and coverage comparisons for home and contents insurance—particularly geared to low-income Australians—would be a start. And policy-makers shouldn't forget the power of a nudge. Text messages or letters to remind people to take out insurance when they move into a new home could drive cost-effective increases in coverage.

Beyond insurers, we face a very real challenge in determining how the costs of climate-change adaptation might be shared between governments, business and individuals. At present, there's no clarity on which levels of government are responsible for adaptation. The Council of Australian Governments (COAG), which brings together the prime minister, state and territory premiers and chief ministers, and the president of the Australian Local Government Association, is the natural forum for this discussion—and some discussion has already taken place there. COAG will need to answer some tricky questions that have barely rated a mention so far in federal parliament.

First, how will Australia fund the adaptation task—especially when adaptation measures might benefit a wide range of public and private interests? The construction of a sea wall benefits individuals whose homes are at risk. It may benefit all three levels of government by protecting schools, libraries, roads and other public facilities. It may benefit insurance companies, who might otherwise have to cover the costs of major flood damage. Banks may also hold mortgages over properties that could be destroyed without the sea wall. So, who should pay for constructing the wall? How could government use different financing models to share the costs among those who benefit from such adaptation measures?

Second, how should governments decide how to use their limited resources, so that our priorities are not determined by those with the loudest voices or deepest pockets? Should Australian governments in 2020 be focused on building a desalination plant in rural South Australia, upgrading an airport runway at risk of flooding in Sydney, or publicly acquiring land in inner-western Melbourne to convert to shaded public parks?

Finally, what new approaches to financing community adaptation might be needed? Drought-stricken communities that need to change their crops, or upgrade their irrigation systems for more intensive rainy seasons, may require government means-tested subsidies or income-contingent loans to assist with their adaptation work. Other nations have floated the idea of a government fighting fund to help finance climate-adaptation spending.

These questions have no easy answers, which makes starting a considered and inclusive community discussion about them all the more vital.

o

For too long the debate about climate change in Australia has been toxic, negative and depressing. Climate action needs consistent, strong, bipartisan support from successive Australian governments. And that requires a majority of Australians who will hold their politicians to account for managing the risks and grasping the opportunities.

Powerful vested interests will always fight climate action. Media organisations, which thrive on conflict, will continue to give unwarranted column inches and airtime to cranky climate sceptics. For some politicians, the temptation to exacerbate public uncertainties for political gain will continue to be too great.

But we are optimistic. In the course of researching and writing this book we spoke many climate scientists. Some have been talking about the links between pollution and global warming for forty years. You might expect them to be a group of very depressed people. Yet, to them, this is the golden era of climate politics. According to data produced by the Lowy Institute, more than four in five Australians favour climate action, even knowing that it will come with a price tag. The same survey also found that three in five Australian want our government to play a global leadership role on climate change. Support for climate action has waxed and waned a little over time but, on balance, it has been remarkably resilient in difficult circumstances—a global financial crisis, and a profoundly partisan national climate debate.

Almost one-third of us have taken part in an environmental event such as a rally or a clean-up campaign over the last five years. Over the same period, one in five Australians voted in an election based on an environmental issue and a similar number gave money to an organisation that protects the environment. Solar panels are now installed in over a million Australian homes: up from just eight thousand in 2007. Nowhere is the disconnect between public action and political inaction more obvious.

But the Lowy data isn't all good news. Even though most Australians believe that climate change is happening, over half of us don't believe that it's being caused by humans. Most believe that climate change won't affect Australia very much.

One challenge is that the story is a complex one. Even eminent climate scientists, exacting as they are, can't provide predictions of specific impacts at specific points in time. Cyclones will be more intense in the future—but scientists can't tell you if your town will fall in their path. There will be more-extreme bushfire days—but they can't tell you if fires will threaten your home. Climate change is weakening and degrading the Great Barrier Reef in five or six different ways, all of which are complicated and difficult to explain.

Furthermore, addressing climate change may involve costs in the short term, economic benefits in the medium term and climatic benefits in the long term. These are the kind of trade-offs that humans are poor at managing. Too often governments, business and individuals avoid costs today and discount future benefits.

○

In the late 1940s, tobacco companies were alerted to evidence that smoking could cause cancer. It wasn't long before academic researchers began publicly to air these concerns. In 1969, a tobacco-industry executive famously penned an internal memo that stated, 'doubt is our product since it is the best means of competing with the body of fact that exists in the mind of the general public.' Despite the mounting scientific evidence linking tobacco with cancer, tobacco companies ploughed on—undertaking a myopic crusade to sow doubt in the minds of the public and prevent government action.

In spite of resistance from the tobacco lobby, the number of people smoking has plummeted since the 1950s. Some people still smoke. But hearts and minds have been won—the community understands the links between smoking and painful, protracted and premature death.

Changing behaviours for the common good in the face of vested interests is possible. We've seen progress in Australia on junk food and gun laws. But it requires strong leadership, a clear explanation of the facts, public funding, engagement with experts and clever campaigning.

If Australia is to tackle climate change, we need well-funded climate science: this seems obvious. But the Climate Commission, which was responsible for bringing together and disseminating independent information to the Australian public, was abolished in 2013. An independent presentation of the science is in the interest of all Australians and warrants ongoing government funding.

Sharing the science of global warming is not going to be enough to promote climate action. Fear, long the crux of much climate-change campaigning, is not doing the job. It gives people the impression that Australia confronts a monstrous problem that is highly uncertain and cannot even be fully described, and which we cannot do anything about. Studies have shown that the emotions people are most likely to associate with climate change include anger, powerlessness and irritation. Is it any wonder?

Frankly discussing the science of climate change, and the risks that we face, is important. But so are solutions, successes and the path forward. We know that pricing carbon reduces pollution. Renewable-energy technology is moving us towards climate solutions much quicker than was expected. And, while climate change is a threat to aspects of life in Australia, the nation already has tools and resources to help us manage the problem.

Climate change needs to be a bigger part of mainstream political discussion. Surveys show overwhelmingly that, of Australians who care climate change, relatively few have the natural environment as their chief concern. Climate change is not just about the environment. Left unchecked, climate change in Australia will have devastating effects on the economy and our health. Some of the most persuasive voices on climate action in other countries are from non-political sectors—in the United States, for example, the military is drawing public attention to the significant threats that climate change poses to national security.

For better or worse, Australians do not have faith in a lot of the people doing most of the talking in our national debate about climate change. Polling data shows that politicians are among the least-trusted authorities on climate-change issues. According to research, the trusted voices are family and friends. So we need to get them speaking up in the conversation about climate.

Person-to-person models of climate education can be replicated in local communities, such as the Climate Reality Project, launched by Al Gore in 2006. Under this model, trained presenters from a cross-section of society—doctors, parents, business people, athletes, musicians, priests and students—deliver presentations to their respective communities about the reality of climate change.

Action on climate is also far more likely to take place if it's clear to individuals that they can make a difference. David Krantz, a psychologist at Columbia University's Center for Research on Environmental Decisions, has found that people become more serious about climate change if they play an active role in tackling it.

The best-selling book *Nudge* highlights how small rewards can promote action. For instance, if households are told on their energy bills that they are consuming more than average, they're likely to reduce their use. If they're using less than average, a smiley face on their bill can prevent an efficient household from becoming complacent. Something as simple as changing an office's default printing option to two-sided can have profound effects. This alone has saved seven million pieces of paper each year at Rutgers University in New Jersey.

We can also help households to conserve energy. Parts of Australia were in the past offered subsidised door-to-door energy-efficiency assessments, and we would like to see this program reactivated. Universities, manufacturing plants and high schools all have large roof spaces and substantial energy needs—they're ideal candidates for medium-scale solar power. Schools and workplaces can build momentum for climate action using the energy savings from their solar investments.

Community energy ownership goes a step further. In Germany, some communities are now completely self-sufficient thanks to renewable-energy co-operatives, which sell surplus electricity back to the grid. Research at the University of St Andrews in Scotland has found that, in addition to positive financial results, community-owned energy projects improve people's attitudes towards renewable energy.

Momentum for similar models is building in Australia, with the first Australian community-energy conference—held in 2014—attracting three hundred attendees. Hepburn Wind, near Daylesford in Victoria, is a trailblazer. Owned by more than nineteen hundred Australians and supported by the state government, the wind farm is feeding energy back into the grid. More than half the owners aren't local, suggesting city slickers will be able to get a slice of the action.

In Scotland, government has got on the front foot by providing low-interest finance and other support for establishing renewable-energy projects. To facilitate more energy-cooperative success stories, Australian governments must provide a stable and conducive regulatory environment.

○

The way we source, process and recall information tends to confirm pre-existing views, and this, too, is a roadblock on the path to climate action. In the future it's likely to be a particular problem in some communities that will be affected by a changing climate—farmers, for example, and Australians living in areas where fossil-fuel industries dominate.

Research by Elke Weber, now a professor of business studies and psychology at Columbia University, found that American farmers' beliefs about temperature and rainfall over seven years aligned with their beliefs about climate change—despite the actual measurements telling a different story. Colleagues of Professor Weber at Columbia have found that attitudes towards climate change are affected by people's perceptions of the current temperature outside. On yet another cold and rainy day in Hobart, Canberra or Melbourne it's easy to forget that the Earth is warming. When change is slow and fluctuating, and when it comes with a cost, many of us go with our gut rather than the science.

Farmers will need to do things differently in the future for Australia's agricultural sector to remain successful. And there are existing initiatives that seek to help them adapt to climate change. The Climate Champion Initiative involves thirty-four farmers who are taking steps in adaptation and sharing knowledge with their peers. In Western Australia, the Farm Business Resilience Program piloted a climate-education model specifically for farmers. While worthy of commendation, these programs have neither the scale nor the scope to convince the majority of Australian farmers to take action on climate change.

Bigger, national organisations such as the National Farmers' Federation, the CSIRO and the Climate Council could push for change at the scale needed. These groups have a shared interest in farmers understanding the specific effects of climate change. Local public forums could help farmers understand the long-term impact on both the climate and their businesses.

Climate action will also be daunting for other Australian workers. Endeavours that substantially contribute to Australia's polluting will be more affected by any action we take. We need to make sure that these people are protected, that we have a just transition to a low-pollution economy. All Australians will share the benefits of climate action, so no group of Australians should unfairly bear the costs.

There's a growing movement to ensure that people with the most to lose from climate change are at the centre of Australia's plans. Practically, this means government investing in training to re-skill workers, and bringing green-energy jobs and investment to areas that are currently most dependent on high-pollution industries (for example, in the Latrobe Valley in Victoria and the Hunter Valley in New South Wales, regions heavily dependent on coal).

○

While Australia has been locked in a bitter ideological conflict over climate change, the rest of the world has moved on. Almost a decade ago, in heading towards climate action, Australia was a pioneer. Today, our nation is a laggard.

Climate change will affect almost everything about our daily life in Australia: the kind of work we do and where we live, how we get to work and whether we go outside for lunch, what we eat and how much it costs. We must address this critical issue now, or by 2040 we will be paying all the costs of acting on climate but have experienced few of the substantial potential benefits that will flow from a wise response.

5

Growth

THE LATE LEE Kuan Yew, founding father of Singapore and an international-relations legend, was not known for his diplomatic turn of phrase. But when the dynamic Southeast Asian leader warned in 1980 that Australia would, without reform, become the 'poor white trash of Asia', it nevertheless caused a stir.

In the thirty-five years that followed, Australia avoided the worst of multiple international economic crises. Our economy grew annually in all but two years, far outstripping growth in most developed economies. It was the beginning of our longest boom, an era of enviable prosperity.

Lee Kuan Yew was a fiercely intelligent global leader. But his failure to foresee Australia's economic future was not surprising. National economies are driven by a complex mix of forces, policies and events that themselves defy forecast. A minimum-wage increase in China can result in more expensive Christmas stockings for children around the globe, subsidies for corn producers in the United States can affect the viability of wind farms in Australia, and loan sharks selling mortgages to Americans who can't afford them can help create banking crises in Iceland and Ireland.

In a world of so much uncertainty, is it even possible to determine economic policies that will drive long-term growth? The short answer is yes. It has to be. The prosperity we enjoy in Australia today is not the result of decisions made last week or last year. The seeds were sown over a generation. Prosperity in 2040 will be, in large part, due to decisions we make today.

The CSIRO, established in 1926, is critical to our modern innovation system. Its founders never lived to see CSIRO scientists help invent WiFi or plastic banknotes. But they knew that innovation mattered. Our modern university system was built in the 1950s. Its creators probably never contemplated that four in ten of today's Year 12 graduates would go on to get a bachelor degree. But they knew that education would be crucial. When Gough Whitlam visited Beijing in the depths of the Cold War, he knew China would be important to Australia's future. But even Gough could probably not have predicted that within forty years China would be by far Australia's largest trading partner.

If past generations of policy-makers had been paralysed by uncertainty, Australia would not be as prosperous as it is today. In this chapter, we identify the drivers of Australia's recent prosperity and consider how they are changing. We've grouped these drivers into three broad categories: policy, people and place. In most cases, the drivers of Australia's longest boom are under pressure and, in many cases, will not drive growth as they have in recent years. To create another long boom, our policies must change.

In striving for continued growth, being a rich country is both a blessing and a curse. Certainly, we start the game a little in front. But we also have a lot to lose. If we want another period of long, sustainable growth, Australia needs to be among the best. And, as we must also expect the unexpected, this chapter is about building an economy that's flexible and resilient in the face of change.

Policy

Neither of us likes the Union Jack in the corner of Australia's national flag. It is anachronistic, and it fails to represent both our Indigenous heritage and the independence of our contemporary democracy. But even progressives like us acknowledge that the British gave us a great economic gift: the democratic and legal institutions that provide a platform for Australian prosperity.

As discussed in the Democracy chapter, development economists, who specialise in answering the thorny question of why some countries are rich and others are not, broadly agree that institutions matter more than anything else in determining whether a country grows sustainably. In setting up its institutions along British lines, Australia inherited a system in which the law generally prevails over money and power. Conflicts are resolved in elections, not wars.

Australian governments have built solid economic institutions on these foundations. We have an independent Reserve Bank, high-performing Treasury departments in Canberra and every capital city, and a properly protected banking system. These institutions set the rules of play for the economy. They help ensure that governments and households save in the good times, so that we have a buffer when things turn bad. At their best, these institutions have helped us avoid economic disasters that would have created poverty and wasted productive lives.

Alongside these institutions, Australian governments have implemented solid, occasionally brilliant, economic policy. Floating the dollar created a more flexible economy. Reducing tariffs and opening Australia up to more competition made our economy more efficient and robust. The Reserve Bank's targeting of inflation has helped manage boom-and-bust cycles. Comparatively low levels of public debt have enabled Australian governments of recent decades to continue supporting people in need as the economy ebbs and flows.

Smart policy and sound institutions mean that any Australian can start a business and be confident that good ideas and hard work, rather than connections to decision-makers and corrupt government officials, will bring them success. Australians and foreigners alike can be confident they will not be subject to punitive or arbitrary taxation, or government expropriation of their assets. Money is safe in the bank, contracts will be enforced and employees will be paid what they're due.

How economic policy and institutions work together was tested during the global financial crisis of 2008 and 2009. It was a test that many other nations failed. In just a few weeks, the federal government created a guarantee for deposits held in Australian banks and a $10 billion stimulus package. This laid the foundation for other interventions, including a $42 billion follow-up package and aggressive interest-rate cuts. The arms of economic policy-making and decision-making worked together with a level of co-operation and decisiveness that is still the envy of the world. Australia emerged virtually unscathed from the worst global economic crisis in sixty years.

When young people are unemployed for long periods, their lives, future earnings and career paths can be altered forever. While Australia has a youth-unemployment problem, it pales in comparison to that of countries like Greece, where six in ten young people are today out of work. Through its deft response to the financial crisis, Australia avoided creating a lost generation.

Our financial system is as robust as it is in large part because Australian governments of all stripes have committed to a process of regular reviews and reform. Three federal assessments over the past forty years have been integral: the 1981 Campbell Report, the 1997 Wallis Report and the 2014 Murray Report. None of these reports were perfect, none perfectly implemented. But they stimulated a national discussion and resulted in important improvements to economic policy. We suggest a regular full review of our financial system roughly every decade, with smaller reviews after the system has been challenged (such as after a market crash or an asset bubble) to take stock of the lessons and to continue the perennial task of developing robust, resilient policy and institutions.

It is often argued that the low-hanging fruit of economic-policy reform—the fast reforms with huge payoffs—has already been picked. Ditching the two-airline policy, reducing tariffs and quotas, and allowing more foreign companies to compete in our market have helped to bring down the cost of living and make Australia's economy produce more with less. But it would be unhelpful and incorrect to be too self-congratulatory about Australia's economic-policy performance in recent years. Some no-brainers remain on the table. We lag on broadband, currently sitting at forty-fourth in the world on average internet speeds. We have fallen behind on climate policy, moving backwards while other countries make the shift to lower-pollution economies. Women remain massively under-represented in business leadership roles and the gender pay gap is widening. Our superannuation rate needs to be increased, so that super is a viable alternative to the pension for more Australians.

We also need to continue to push for more openness in Australia's economy. The countries that will prosper over the next twenty-five years will be resilient and competitive. For generations, we have seen global forces buffet Australian farmers and manufacturers. Now, it is businesses in our local shopping strips—chemists, bookstores, clothing stores—which are threatened by international rivals that can provide goods at a lower cost, with fast delivery to our homes (in the case of books and music, in an instant).

Because the threshold for openness and competitiveness continues to rise, we need to keep pushing merely to keep pace with the rest of the world. If reforms make our economy and our businesses more efficient, we should be biased towards undertaking them, even if the payoffs are more marginal than they have been in the past. Over the years, organisations such as the Productivity Commission have identified scores of possible reform areas to improve Australia's competitiveness. The list is long and the proposals are politically tough. Some may not be worth the economic payoff but, broadly, the reforms are moderate yet important.

Clearly, there is a reform agenda ahead, but few quick wins remain. Many of Australia's biggest long-term economic challenges sit outside traditional economic portfolios. What will be our future equivalent to floating the dollar? For the coming generation, decisions made by the Minister for Early Childhood Education, for Asian Engagement or for Climate Change could have a greater influence on long-term growth than those made by the treasurer.

o

One potentially heavy-hitting reform—over which there is vigorous debate—is the role of government in building a high-skill, high-wage economy. Australia should have thriving exports in education, financial services, complex machinery, high fashion, medical devices and patented technology, as well as what we dig out of the ground and grow in the earth. An educated population is a necessary piece of the puzzle, but we need high-skill jobs and industries to get the best out of a high-skill workforce. And we can create more of them without spending any additional taxpayer dollars.

Most economics textbooks would say that government has nothing to do with innovation. But real-world evidence—and examples from global success stories such as Finland and Israel—suggests otherwise. In a digital economy, government policy that favours innovation and entrepreneurship makes a big difference. Not through command and control, and not just through tweaking the operation of markets, but by government engaging where it can have an effect: bringing a strategic approach to national innovation, connecting different parts of the economy so we are more than the sum of our parts, and supporting plucky individuals with great ideas.

Australia has a history of innovation and invention. Evidence abounds, from the woomera to Australian Rules football, the stump-jump plough to the bionic ear, spray-on skin to plastic money. There are many more mundane but important innovations that never make the papers: manufacturing processes that use less waste, payment systems that allow people to bank more quickly.

But the road ahead looks rocky. Professor Ian Chubb has reported that, in 2011, 1.5 per cent of Australian businesses created innovations that were genuinely new to the world, compared to 10 to 40 per cent in leading OECD countries. Economists at Harvard University and MIT use an Economic Complexity Index to predict future growth in nations around the world. The index predicts growth based on a nation's diversity (how many things a country makes) and specialisation (how deeply expert a nation is in those areas). It is a better predictor of growth than any other model economists use, and it suggests that Australia's exports are both too narrow and too thin to justify expectations of strong growth in the coming years.

These are not the only indicators that we do not have our innovation policies quite right. Spending on research and development (R&D) is below the OECD average. Collaboration between industries and the scientific-research sector is far too low—for large businesses, at 90 per cent in the Finland, 40 per cent in Norway and 4 per cent in Australia. Successive governments have chopped and changed on innovation policy, leaving many in industry bewildered.

Australia is a relatively small country. With just 2 per cent of the world's R&D spend, we cannot be a leader in everything. Yet, today, Australia's innovation spending is spread across a dazzling array of initiatives and projects. Professor Ian Chubb has argued that Australia must articulate national research priorities to focus our spending. He has observed that there are now ten thousand firms listed for the R&D Tax Incentive and each may be funded to research different topics. Government spending is similarly diffuse. In 2013, there were seventy-nine R&D lines in the federal budget, ranging over fourteen ministerial portfolios.

It is not just in R&D spending where a more strategic approach could make our dollars go further. Australia's innovation spending includes a much broader set of government-funded programs and institutions: university research funding, scientific research, CSIRO projects. Regulation is another way that we influence innovation—for example, policies like the Renewable Energy Target offer incentives to innovate in renewable energies—again, with little strategy for how regulation supports spending and vice versa.

Economics students may bristle at the idea of government driving specialisation. A maxim taught in first-year economics in universities around the world is that governments should not pick winners. But government spending in Australia is 35 per cent of GDP. Where governments put that money inevitably shapes our economy. In some instances, government interventions are direct, such as determining to build submarines bought by our defence forces offshore instead of in Australia. Sometimes they are less direct: how many students we fund each year to study biochemistry, or whether we build a new freeway in Gladstone or Geelong. Every time governments allocate a dollar to one sector over another, or negotiate a trade agreement that will be tougher on one product than another, they pick a winner. Without a strategic approach, governments still make strategic decisions. They're just probably not very good ones.

In 2013, the McKinsey Global Institute released a report on Australia's economic future, 'Compete to Prosper'. The authors found that almost 70 per cent of industry assistance goes to industries that are in decline, where Australia arguably doesn't have a comparative advantage. Some of these industries are critical regardless and need ongoing support. But, overall, we would benefit from a national debate about how we could reorient these investments towards our strengths—including goods and services that will best position Australia to partner with Asia. Government funding should back the spear-carriers, not the pallbearers.

There are a couple of caveats on bringing a strategic approach to innovation policy: first, we need to ensure that we don't inadvertently stifle creativity in unexpected areas. Innovation, technology and invention are unpredictable beasts. Some broad-based funding must remain in place, and we must continue to provide strong support for basic research. (Research without a specific goal in mind, which can be very lucrative. It's how the CSIRO helped invent WiFi.) A further and real danger with a more strategic approach is that the strategy may be politicised. Innovation policy could become a new form of protectionism, looking after established interests with powerful stakeholders, rather than industries with huge potential but little political sway.

In these matters, we will have to engage and trust experts and institutions. Israel has put its chief scientist at the centre of the nation's innovation system. Vinnova, an innovation agency, is at the heart Sweden's system; Sitra plays a similar role in Finland. These countries are long-term global innovation leaders.

Regardless of the model Australia adopts across innovation and entrepreneurship, some semblance of bipartisanship will be required for it to be successful. Clare has a close-up perspective on how constant policy change is affecting businesses. She represents a manufacturing region, and the reaction to the Rudd government's manufacturing innovation hub at Monash University was an early warning. It was good policy: strategic, focused on an area of regional strength, in line with global thinking on best practices. While many local businesses joined the hub, the challenge was getting them to actively engage. The word from manufacturers was that they'd seen it all before, and believed it wouldn't last. (And it didn't. The program was effectively dismantled in 2014.) We need to restore trust in the business community so that Australian governments can get the policy settings right—and stick to them.

Commercialisation is a further riddle. While we are an innovative country, evidence suggests that we are not so good at turning our clever ideas into flourishing businesses. Patenting activity is low in

Australia compared to other countries. We have far fewer start-ups and fewer entrepreneurs. And as a consequence much less of our national wealth is coming from inventions and new ideas. These contribute about 0.5 per cent of our GDP, compared with 3 per cent in Sweden.

It's through commercialisation that Australia will reap economic benefits from innovation and invention. So we need to build a culture more encouraging of start-ups and entrepreneurs, one where taking risks—and failing—is accepted as a regular part of business. Some may think that government has no role in making this happen, but a quick look at the evidence will put the assumption to bed.

One factor is quality entrepreneurship training. Innovative models combining education, mentoring and networking are popping up around the nation. The University of Melbourne's Accelerator Program supports and educates young entrepreneurs, and is showing signs of early success. Capital Markets CRC in Sydney aims to turn great ideas from the academy into commercial success. The company started with a seed grant from government. Today, they are almost financially independent and have established their own venture capital fund. Under the leadership of entrepreneur and chief scientist Michael Aitken, they also host a world-class program for doctoral students that turns some of Australia's smartest PhD graduates into entrepreneurs. They recruit thirty PhDs every year. For each young person who returns to university after completing the program, two stay in the private sector to invent and commercialise great ideas. So far, the organisation has been the engine of a dozen great ideas and six spin-off companies.

We've discussed a handful of the ways in which government can get better returns on our innovation dollars, but there are many others. This is a fast-evolving area where even global leaders are still working out the ideal role for government in digital, innovation-led economic growth. But Australia has a long way to go to be the best in class. That much is apparent, even today.

People

With solid institutions, fair and efficient rules, and the right incentives in place, Australia's prosperity is largely about its people: how many there are, how many are working and how good they are at what they do. Over the past thirty years, Australia has improved in each of these areas.

Over recent decades, baby boomers—the largest of Australia's generations—were in the most productive part of their working lives. But the country's demographics are changing. By 2040, the number of people over sixty-five will have doubled, and the number over eighty-five will have tripled. The boomers will be between eighty and ninety-five years old, no longer working, and require pensions, aged care and more acute medical assistance.

Older Australians will continue to make a contribution, economic and otherwise. But this is going to be an expensive period in the life of the nation. The impact on government budgets is broadly understood. The cost of pensions alone will almost triple to 2040. Adding to this are superannuation tax concessions, which are set to outstrip the size of the aged pension by the end of this decade.

Ensuring that every Australian who wants to work can do so will help us manage the costs of ageing. There is a large group of highly educated people who have not yet been tapped to their full economic potential: Australian women. Their entry into the workforce has been a very significant driver of recent growth in Australian household incomes over the last generation. Australia would be a much poorer country today if a woman's place was in the home.

Despite this trend, female workforce participation in Australia is still lower—at 59 per cent—than in many other countries. The Grattan Institute has estimated that up to twenty-five billion dollars in annual economic activity could be generated if we bring the participation of Australian women up to the level seen in Canada. This is a bigger reform payoff than policy areas that receive much more attention, such as tax reform.

There are obvious reasons why some women aren't realising their economic potential. The nation faces tremendous problems with quality, affordable child care. The complex web of taxes, family payments, and child-care costs and subsidies means that some women on the minimum wage take home $3.50 per hour. Many women make the rational decision that going back to work doesn't make economic sense.

In Australia today, women working full-time are paid on average 18 per cent less than men, and—as the economics editor of Melbourne's *Age* pointed out earlier this year—'companies run by a Peter, a Michael, a David or an Andrew outnumber those run by women four to one.' If we can help women to take their rightful place in boardrooms, in courtrooms and at cabinet tables around the country, all Australians will benefit.

Comprehensive reporting of gender wage gaps and the share of female leadership in all public companies, and maintaining lists of eminent, qualified Australian women for vacant board positions, are good places to start. Government should set the example by meeting aggressive affirmative-action targets. But if the business community won't move with a little bit of prodding, government will need to go further and use the law.

Women are not the only means of building a larger workforce. Immigration is another way in which Australia can manage the effects of an ageing population, though it is not a panacea. Even if Australia brings two hundred thousand migrants into our country every year, we will end up with 2.7 workers for every non-worker by 2050, compared to 4.5 today. (With a zero-migration program, we will end up with two workers for every non-worker—placing the huge task of paying for ageing on fewer shoulders.) A larger migration intake of three hundred thousand people per annum would result in three workers for every non-worker.

Such a solution has merit, but also comes with a hitch. Australia is not the only country looking for young, skilled migrants. Canada, the United States, New Zealand and the United Kingdom—all attractive destinations—will be vying for the best talent, especially from Asia. At the same time, as Asia becomes more prosperous more potential migrants might be inclined to stay where they are. And more young Australians may leave for Asia. Australia will have to compete to attract the workers it needs.

Young migrants create welcoming communities, encouraging further migrant flows. We should encourage this now, not wait until we—and every other developed country—are desperate. Increasing our skilled migration numbers also gives migrants time to settle down, to develop the professional and business connections they need to build prosperity for their families and for our nation. An essential part of making immigration a success is better planning in our cities. If we can't make our cities work with extra people, public support for immigration will evaporate.

Another source of migrants is the world's eighteen million refugees. Many wait for years in formal and informal refugee camps, their economic potential wasting away. Anyone unsure about the economic contribution of refugees should visit our electorates, in southeast and western Melbourne. Our areas hum with the entrepreneurial skills and talent of first- and second-generation migrants, many of whom arrived as refugees. They tell us that Australia has given them a second chance and they have grabbed it with both hands.

o

Even with a larger population and improved participation rates, we will still end up with more retired people as a share of the population than we have ever seen. To grow the economy, Australian workers are going to have to do more with less.

In this, education and skills will be paramount. The skills of Australia's population have driven economic growth through our longest boom, and they will matter even more to 2040. Our economy is changing, with greater demand for highly educated workers (who will create more economic value). A better-educated population will help Australia attract and expand high-skill industries: education, technology, financial services, advanced manufacturing.

If we can meet the challenge of better educating our population, the economic benefits will be huge. For individuals, an extra year of education can increase annual wages up to 16 per cent. Raising the average level of education by one year across the economy as a whole is associated with 3 to 15 per cent higher GDP growth. Educated populations get more out of everyone in the economy: educated workers raise the productivity level of people around them, great managers get a lot more out of their staff and, in a more educated workforce, workers think of better ways to work, all the time.

For all that we can't know about Australia's economic future, we are confident about this: if Australia wants continued prosperity, it needs to be among the best-educated countries in the world.

A child starting prep this year will enter the workforce in the mid- to late 2030s; a Year 10 student will be mid-career by 2040. We need to prepare young people for a 2040 economy, not a 2015 economy. By 2040, the ability to create and use technology will determine the wages of many workers. They'll be competing in a labour market that's ever more global. Australia's economy will be dwarfed by the Asian economies that surround us. To be relevant, many more of our workers will need to understand the region intimately. And the most successful workers of the future will love learning, as they will likely need to return to formal and informal education throughout their lives. To remain a high-skill, high-wage economy, Australia will need to stay ahead of the pack. And the pack is moving fast.

There are some spectacular things happening in schools across the country. In good schools, team teaching is embedded in classrooms, lesson plans are individually crafted around student needs and the process of learning is being discussed with children, even in their first years of primary school. These teaching methods are world's-best practice.

On average, though, Australia's system is in relative decline. NAPLAN, which measures children's literacy and numeracy in Years 3, 5, 7 and 9, shows that our school system is not getting better at teaching over time.

While Australia still compares favourably with most other major developed countries, on global assessments we're starting to look mediocre—nineteenth on maths, thirteenth on English, and moving south. The nations leaving us behind are predominantly Asian. In the most recent PISA tests (which allow us to compare school systems across the world) the top-seven maths performers were Asian countries. And we can't just excuse these results by arguing that Asian students are good rote learners. Even in PISA problem-solving tests, which challenge students with unstructured problems, Asian nations dominate. What's happening in classrooms across Shanghai and Singapore—the two global leaders in education—is evidence of a radical transformation of Asian school systems. (Though Australia is not just getting left behind by Asia. We also lag behind Canada, Poland, Finland and a number of other European countries.)

If Australia is still to have a high-skill, high-wage economy in 2040, we need to ask ourselves a difficult question. What will Australian students be able to do in a generation that our global competitors—especially our Asian neighbours—won't be able to do better, faster, cheaper?

Unlike demographics, over which policy-makers have limited control, education is fundamentally about good public policy. School systems around the world can and do make fast turnarounds. There are many proposals for reform, plenty of expertise in Australia about what works and what doesn't, and a vast amount of data to help us undertake reform. The challenge is to work out, of all the proposals, where to focus our efforts.

Most of us have had some spectacular teachers in our lives. In Year 11, politics became Clare's passion because Mr Farnsworth threw out the curriculum and brought Australian politics to life with superb impromptu lectures on everything from the Dismissal to the history of Australian Indigenous policy. In the debates we've had in Australia about how to improve our education system, there is a simple message that sometimes gets lost: teachers matter most.

This is the core finding of years of research into why some children learn a lot in some classrooms and not much in others. Exceptional teaching is at the heart of the world's highest-performing school systems. Australian teachers are, by and large, excellent at what they do. We're asking them to go beyond that and be the best in the world. And to achieve that, we are going to need to make some changes and provide them with a lot more support to do what they love.

Australian teachers are the harshest critics of our current model of teacher training. A recent Australian Institute of Teaching and School Leadership survey indicated that a third of early career secondary teachers found their training unhelpful in teaching numeracy, involving parents and guardians, and teaching Aboriginal and Torres Strait Islander students. Principals weren't rapt, either, reporting that only 10 to 15 per cent of graduate secondary teachers came well prepared in teaching students with disabilities and dealing with difficult student behaviour.

Teacher education varies from country to country and there is no one model that we should be seeking to emulate. But, in systems with the best results, classrooms are places of learning for teachers as well as for students. In many world-class systems, teaching is seen and taught as a craft. Mastering that craft is a career-long goal, not something to be achieved in a few years while at university. In Shanghai, teachers learn largely on the job, through an apprenticeship model. Apprentices are taught by a master teacher, who is relieved of much of their regular duties for a year while they train their protégé. The master observes and provides intense coaching, illustrating best practice through their own performance.

High-performing systems usually combine on-the-job training with a strong culture of ongoing research, feedback and improvement—even for the most senior teachers. In Shanghai, teachers must be versed in current research, and to qualify for senior teaching positions must have published papers and be vetted by an expert committee. In the United Kingdom, more schools are employing 'research leads', who assist colleagues in using evidence to improve their teaching.

Australians will be asking for more from their teachers, and we need to recognise that with better pay and prestige. Teachers in Australia have a good starting salary compared with their international counterparts, but as they become more expert they don't have much room to move. If we want Australia's best and brightest to spend their professional careers developing our most precious national resource, we must significantly increase teacher pay, especially for our best performers. And, if we expect teachers to integrate research and ongoing learning into their everyday role, they will need more time. Most teachers work tremendously hard, racing from classes to meetings throughout the day, and supervising activities before and after school. Anyone who's spent extended periods of time around kids knows that keeping twenty-five of them on track for a whole day is a tough ask. One option in this respect is for junior support staff to take on the more routine elements of school life.

○

It's often hoped that technology will free up teachers for more ongoing learning and planning, collaborating and feedback. Certainly, we're seeing a technological transformation in the delivery of education. The Khan Academy, Coursera and other Massive Open Online Courses (online institutions that provide courses—sometimes from Harvard, MIT and other world-class universities—free to anyone with an internet connection) are allowing millions of people to learn from some of the world's best teachers. Forty per cent of Coursera users come from developing nations. In time, the equity implications of this shift could be significant.

What's less clear is how technology might integrate with, or replace, parts of our current teaching system to 2040. Online learning has already shaken up universities—ask any parent with a twenty-year-old who watches most of their lectures from the family-room couch. But how far will these changes go? Will we still have classrooms in 2040? Will gaming or holograms play a role? Will personalised interactive lesson plans be generated by complex algorithms, classrooms cross over national boundaries and celebrity teachers instruct millions by video?

We can't know the answers to these questions. But we know that good teachers who think creatively about technology will be at the forefront of developments. Teachers will remain essential, because they will be the experts and researchers in how to build new educational models around seismic technological developments, whatever they may be. And because computers, games and videos will not be able to teach kids how to sit still, organise themselves, debate ideas with others students and work in teams—to try, fail and try again.

○

As an MP, while living in remote Northern Australia and as a local mayor, Clare has visited more than one hundred Australian schools. Some are beautiful, others crumbling; some classrooms are vibrant and hum with productivity, others are staid and flat. Sometimes Australian schools just a few hundred metres apart vary wildly in improving student learning. If we are going to get to world-class level, this is going to have to change.

Nations that have consistently performed well by international standards—including Finland, Korea and Canada—have a narrow distribution of student performance, meaning there is a small education gap between high- and low-performing students. In the best systems, all boats rise together, with socioeconomic background playing a minimal role in educational outcome. But that's not what we see in Australia at present.

Funding schools according to the need of the student body is a sound, basic principle that drove David Gonski's famous report into equity in Australia's school system. Reforms that align funding with student needs simply must be implemented.

No one has argued that money alone will solve all the equity problems in our schools. Some schools that today receive similar funding achieve very different student outcomes. Analysis of NAPLAN scores in the *Australian* indicates that between 10 and 25 per cent of our schools have low-scoring students who see little academic improvement over time. Students at these schools come disproportionally from socioeconomically disadvantaged backgrounds. Alongside Gonski, a fast, effective way to lift Australia's performance is to take the worst-performing schools, many of which serve our most disadvantaged students, and bring them up to average.

This isn't just a cause that egalitarians should get behind: serious money is on the line. The OECD has estimated that raising the results of the bottom tenth of Australian students to a minimum four-hundred-point score in international PISA tests would deliver significantly faster growth, and an additional two trillion US dollars of GDP between today and 2090. That's more than twice the size of Australia's economy. It's a modest education target with a big economic windfall.

Improving academic outcomes for low-achieving disadvantaged students will get more young Australians to a crucial educational milestone: graduating from Year 12. Getting more students to this point will raise incomes, drive down underemployment and unemployment, reduce the pressure on welfare and government services, and lower the likelihood of individuals being caught in the justice system. Concentrating on low-performing, needy schools—in parallel with a fairer method of funding—is our best bet in unlocking additional human capital.

We know that improvement in these schools is possible. Bright Spots is the term Social Ventures Australia uses for schools that buck the trend to deliver educational outcomes significantly above what their community profile would suggest. Over time, governments at different levels have implemented turnaround strategies for relatively small numbers of schools, often successfully. But we need to generate change on a larger scale.

We do know a few things that are *not* the solution to poor school performance. Attempting to improve the American system by injecting more competition and school choice has so far yielded few gains: the United States is well below Australia in global rankings. The American approach of relying on market mechanisms also won't take care of our social-justice concerns. Market mechanisms require parents to fight for their kids to attend a great school. The system should work hardest for students whose parents are least likely to vote with their feet.

London has taken a different and successful approach to narrowing the achievement gap across a whole school system. Since its school-turnaround program began in 2000, the number of underperforming schools has fallen, the number judged outstanding has risen, and the gap between the results of low- and high-socioeconomic-background students has shrunk.

Significant effort was put into developing a moral case for change, drawing on evidence of the extent of underperformance among disadvantaged schools to generate a sense of urgency. Educators took pride in their role in meeting this moral challenge, feeling they had the backing of the community due to additional resourcing, and the sustained involvement of leaders from government and the education sector.

Extra resources were devoted to improving school facilities, raising teacher pay and, most importantly, providing a dedicated team of experts to work closely with schools. This led to a sense that this was not business as usual, enhanced by beginning new initiatives, including the prestigious teacher-training program Teach First and the creation of academies—new schools with a fresh, high-performance culture. These changes improved the previously poor image of London schools, assisting the recruitment and retention of teachers and principals. While all schools were supported, encouraged and advised by teams of experts, authority remained with teaching staff and principals. This encouraged pride in success and ownership of problems that occurred along the way.

A new culture of data-driven action and evaluation is also credited with lifting results. London schools were supported in developing the capacity to collect and understand data, and this in turn enabled a forensic focus on effectiveness in the classroom. It was the basis for increased accountability and challenging poor performance, which previously may have been suspected but not quantified. Finally, schools weren't expected to go it alone. Advisers, policy-makers and academics were engaged and worked together for their schools as a united force.

Just as important is drawing on the know-how of our high-performing schools. Shanghai uses a model where underperforming schools are partnered with the highest-performing ones, and the two schools' leaders are required to work together to improve performance, sharing teachers, good practices and leadership coaching. A high-performing school receives additional funding if they succeed in improving the lower-ranked school's performance.

○

Pick out a random person on the street and they will be able to tell you that Australia's economic future lies in Asia. Yet, after more than a decade of opinion pieces, there are fewer students studying Asian languages in Australia today than there were in 2000. Ben Jensen at the Grattan Institute has calculated that only 6 per cent of Australian students study an Asian language, and many of these are from Asian backgrounds. Whatever policies we've tried, they're not working.

Here are a few pieces of the puzzle—ways we can improve. Within a decade, scale back government funding for French, Spanish and Italian in Australian primary schools, and make learning at least one Asian language compulsory. Train some of the thousands of Australians who are bilingual in an Asian language to fill teaching gaps. And create a new federal exchange program to triple the number of young secondary students who spend a year studying in Asia.

Australia's education system is not wanting for good reform ideas. Getting to the level of exceptional in education is a matter of prioritisation. We can do it—but only if it's one of the top priorities of successive Australian governments from now until 2040. We want Liberal and Labor to make a gutsy bipartisan commitment to do what it will take to get Australia into the top-three education systems in the world by 2040. If in a generation we're explaining to our children why they're not enjoying increased prosperity, a failure of Australian governments to prioritise education will be the most likely culprit.

o

There's a lot more to a high-skill, high-wage economy than we've talked about here. In a short book, we haven't made room to discuss higher education, lifelong learning, on-the-job training, apprenticeships and many other elements of policy. These areas are vitally important. But if we can't get Australia's education and innovation policies right, the other policies won't help much in surfing the tidal wave of technological, global and competitive change that's making its way towards us quickly.

Place

The first British arrivals to Australia had a fraught relationship with the land. Accounts from the time express anger and frustration with hot and dusty conditions, while the cloudy, cool climate of the motherland was idealised. Little did the colonists know that land would be at the heart of our national prosperity centuries on. Australia has significant endowments shared among a small population. With abundant natural resources and arable soil, a pristine natural environment and a position at the edge of the world's fastest-growing region, our place in the world will continue to matter immensely to growth in the years to 2040.

In recent times, mining has been an important driver of prosperity. Before the resources boom, about ten out of every hundred dollars of Australia's nominal GDP came from mining or closely related fields, and this doubled at the height of the recent ireon-ore boom.

But booms don't last and, when we look at international data, the evidence clearly shows that resources alone do not deliver long-term prosperity. Some studies show a negative correlation between resources exports and growth. On average, the more a country exports natural resources, the slower that country is likely to grow.

Mining has risks and downsides. In 1959, a huge gas discovery in the Netherlands led to a thriving gas-export industry. Soon after, other parts of the national economy began to struggle. 'Dutch disease' has since become shorthand for the effect of a resources boom on currency: when a nation's exports rise, its currency increases in value, making other export industries (manufacturing and agriculture, in Australia's case) more expensive to sell overseas.

Between 2003 and 2013, the price of iron ore tripled, and mining investment rose from 2 to 8 per cent of Australia's GDP. This—and the inevitable comedown—is a radical economic change for a country to absorb in a short time. Mining profits also tend to go offshore. In Australia, our minerals are mostly mined by huge global companies that are majority foreign-owned. In Australia's recent mining boom, about two-thirds of profits went to foreign shareholders.

None of this is to say that mineral resources are bad for Australia's economy. Millions of Australians benefit from ownership of company shares, royalties paid to Australian governments, direct employment and the indirect gains from living in a country where some are getting rich from resources. But politicians and businesses need to be frank about who gains and who loses from the exploitation of our natural resources. Our incredible national mineral endowment will only deliver long-term growth if we have the right policies in place—that much is clear from the international evidence. Otherwise, we pay the costs of living in a resources economy but don't get the benefits.

Some basic principles should guide policy-making. Australia's minerals belong to all Australians, not to mining companies. But mining companies take risks to find and exploit minerals, and that risk must be rewarded. Our minerals are non-renewable: once gone, they are gone forever. Logically, we should use the fruits of resources booms to invest in long-term growth and resilience.

Looking ahead to 2040, mining will continue to play a role in our national economy, though how significantly we cannot know for sure. According to Geoscience Australia, the country has the largest economically significant deposits of iron ore, gold, lead, rutile, zircon, nickel, uranium and zinc in the world. It also ranks in the top six for ten other non-renewable resources.

There will likely be plenty of demand for these resources. The United Nations predicts a global population of nine billion people by 2040. Asia's middle classes will expect more lavish lifestyles. Energy needs in the region will rise. But, beyond these obvious assertions, we can do no more than speculate. Natural gas is likely to grow significantly in the short term, though by 2040 export volumes are likely to have levelled off. China's policy ambition is to triple its existing nuclear-energy capacity, with twenty-four nuclear-power reactors currently under construction and more planned. Other nations may urbanise, driving new demand for iron ore. Renewable energies and cars using battery storage could lead to an explosion in demand for lithium. We can't predict the specifics. But we can be confident that, for Australia, mining will continue to matter.

There is disagreement among economists and policy-makers about Australia's ongoing management of the resources boom. Did monetary policy effectively manage inflation and the exchange rate? How did benefits from the boom differ among high- and low-skilled workers? Did skills gaps constrain growth during the boom? What were the net benefits of the boom for non-mining sectors? Did we balance profits flowing offshore with benefits for Australians? These are complex questions that have been highly politicised, to the point where any government that attempts policy change is unlikely to be able to build community consensus. We need a fact base. We suggest that the Productivity Commission conduct a thorough post-mortem, analysing the evidence of how Australian governments managed the recent boom and recommending how to manage future booms.

Even without this information, there are several aspects of Australia's policy response during the boom that have obvious room for improvement. Australian governments did not collect enough in tax from mining companies as commodity prices rose. Between 2000 and 2005, total taxes and royalties as a share of mining profits was almost 40 per cent. As prices rose in the back half of the decade, the figure fell to less than 20 per cent—lower, according to some reports.

A share of the additional revenues collected during the recent boom was used to set up a Future Fund to finance public-servant superannuation liabilities and some smaller long-term investments. Some additional revenue was used to improve Australia's fiscal position. But many billions were treated as though they would last forever, locked into future budgets through tax cuts and new recurrent spending, fuelling the everyday expenses of the nation. We're paying for it today, as commodity prices return to historically normal levels and we tackle a national revenue shortfall.

How can we keep governments informed and honest about these matters, so that we don't in future bake one-off revenues into our recurrent budgets? Sunlight, as they say, is the best disinfectant. We argue for full transparency: we need independent advice on what share of mining tax revenues is sustainable and what is not; about how each share is being invested, saved or spent, and on what. And we have plenty of international models to choose from.

Chile, famous for its football and wine, is also a world leader in managing natural resources. It has a novel institutional approach to splurging one-off boom revenues on pre-election sweeteners. Two independent panels use expert knowledge to assess how the output and price of copper (Chile's key natural endowment) correspond to their respective long-run values. Using these judgments, a target is set for the overall budget balance. When times are good—copper prices are high and output is above trend—Chile saves by running a budget surplus, and when times a bad the country runs a deficit. The panels are independent of the political process, and include representatives from mining companies, the financial sector, research institutions and universities.

Models like this aren't perfect—even expert panels get things wrong. But we need to find better ways to bring transparency to Australia's resources policy-making. If there's one lesson from the recent boom, it's that we need to get the policy right before the next boom is upon us.

o

In 1964, just before the start of the Cultural Revolution that would leave China's people poor and starving, a boy named Jack Ma was born in Hangzhou, China. According to legend, Ma didn't use a computer or the internet until he was over thirty. Two decades later, he's the richest man in China. In 2014, Ma floated Alibaba.com on the New York Stock Exchange. At the time, it was the biggest initial public offering ever seen. Alibaba.com is worth three times as much as BHP Billiton, Australia's largest company and the world's biggest mining company. Ma's business connects millions of customers and sellers from around the world in a thriving online wholesale marketplace. Alibaba.com could provide a gateway for Australian businesses to buy from and sell to China.

Jack Ma's story illustrates how quickly things are changing in China—and that Australia's economic engagement with that nation is going to be on their terms, not ours. Most Australians have never heard of Jack Ma or perhaps even Alibaba.com, and if we are to get the most out of being located in the world's fastest-growing region this has to change.

The amazing economic growth of Asian nations has driven much of Australia's recent growth. Our three largest export destinations are China, Japan and South Korea, paying fifty-six of every one hundred dollars of goods and services we export. Asia as a whole is our biggest customer.

Growth in Asia has largely fuelled demand for our resources and the higher prices we've received for them. In recent years, this has been due to demand for iron ore, for all the steel in the office blocks, apartments, warehouses, factories and bridges that fast-urbanising countries build.

Some economists estimate that China and India alone will account for more than half of all global economic output by 2040. If we throw in Japan, Vietnam and the Asian Tigers—Hong Kong, Singapore, South Korea and Taiwan—two-thirds of every dollar of wealth created globally by 2040 will come from our region.

More than two million Chinese millionaires are in the market for wealth-management services, a rising middle class will seek the best education for its children, families will want great holiday destinations, an ageing population will need care providers. These are some of the opportunities for Australia.

But making the most of these opportunities is far from a fait accompli. We are close to Asia, but not that close. As Treasury Secretary Martin Parkinson has pointed out, Beijing is closer to Berlin than it is to Brisbane. We have already mentioned the disappointing engagement with Asian languages in our schools. Just as worryingly, according to a recent PricewaterhouseCoopers (PwC) report, 'Passing Us By', only 9 per cent of Australian companies are doing business in Asia.

It's not as if Australian businesses have an aversion to conducting business overseas. China has three hundred times as many people as New Zealand, yet PwC's analysis shows that Australian companies invested about seven times as much money in New Zealand in 2014 as they did in China. The PwC report also shows that Australian businesses are much more reticent than other foreign investors—American and European engagement with Asia dwarfs Australia's. We are already getting left behind.

Asia is not just Australia's customer: it is also a competitor. Asian brands are buying up dairy farms and commercial property in Australia, and selling tech goods through Lenovo and Huwei. As a new generation of lawyers, financiers and other professionals are training in Asia, our service industries are coming under pressure, too. Asia is reaching out to us. If we don't reach back, we risk being little more than a quarry and a pasture for our rapidly growing neighbours.

PwC's report suggests that Australian companies succeeding in Asia today arrived there fifteen years ago. It takes time to understand Asian consumers, work through logistics and build trusting business relationships. Yet fund managers punish executives and boards who invest outside Australia's cosy oligopolies. With an average tenure of

4.2 years, CEOs are unlikely to reap the benefits of taking a risk on Asia, and our boards lack deep expertise in Asian business. Certainly, some companies are making the leap. But getting growth from Asia is going to take a lot of hard work.

Business will be in the driver's seat, but government will play its role. Governments negotiate trade agreements, influencing how competitive Australian goods are in overseas markets. Australian governments should be trying to gain deeper access to Asian markets. But not all trade agreements are created equal, and the current process is not sufficiently strategic, robust or focused on long-term growth.

While theory suggests otherwise, in reality trade agreements create winners and losers. We need to be careful that these trade-offs are made to serve Australia's long-term future as a high-skill, high-wage economy. A trade agreement that gains great access to Asian markets for primary products but makes adverse changes to intellectual property laws, or reduces the competitiveness of our complex manufacturing or medical devices, may not be in the national interest.

Today, there is no agreed, transparent set of objectives guiding Australia's negotiations. Free-trade agreements—hard as it is to believe—are often not fully modelled for their impact on Australia's economy. It should be standard for complete quantitative analyses to be done on trade agreements, so that we know what we are signing up for.

Globally, trade agreements are becoming more creative, and there could be opportunities to use these negotiations to help Australian businesses. Recent accords between China and India, for example, offer incentives for Chinese companies to manufacture goods in India in specially zoned industrial parks. The two countries are also sharing data to better manage flooding of the Brahmaputra River on a border between the countries, and working together to train officials.

o

When we talk to exporters, there's a recurring theme: doing business in Asia is hard. Because of the language barrier, conversations about sensitive matters take a long time, there are frequent misunderstandings, and—without personal and family connections—hearing about business opportunities is a challenge. There are cultural differences between regions. Trust, so central to trading relationships, is tough to establish.

To get the most out of the economic opportunities in the region, Australians need to engage with Asia one person at a time, like twenty-four million tentacles reaching out from our shores and into the region: online and through travel, cultural exchange, teaching, shared interests.

Our close relationship with Britain rests on centuries of engagement: camaraderie in the trenches, rivalries on the sporting field, wave upon wave of migration, and enjoyment of one another's culture—from *War Horse* to the Australian Ballet, *The Bill* to *Neighbours*. We need to build the same kind of links with China and other Asian nations. But we have just one generation in which to do it. The 'Australia in the Asian Century' White Paper, published in 2012, remains an excellent blueprint from which to work.

We're not beginning this task from a standing start. Two hundred and sixty thousand people from Asia study in our universities each year; more than 2.8 million Asian visitors saw our sights or conducted business in Australia in 2013. But we have work to do, starting with our democratic institutions. The proportion of our population that was born in Asia is now about 10 per cent, with more people claiming Asian ancestry—yet only a handful of members of parliament are Asian Australian. Government boards—those which determine Research Council grants, research and development investment, regulation of health and aged care—must bring skilled Asian Australians onto their boards. We're not talking about quotas, but about government departments and decision-makers recognising the value of such a move and maintaining a list of eligible people for consideration.

We need to continue to attract Asian students to our universities. We would like to see a sister school in Asia for each Australian primary and secondary school, with exchange programs and weekly Skype chats. Engagement in science and research between the two countries will help, using organisations like the Australian Research Council.

Australia's diaspora communities will be a huge asset in the task. There are almost three hundred thousand members of the Indian diaspora living here, but our trading relationship with India falls a long way short of its potential. Who better to help Australia engage with one of the largest and fastest-growing markets in the world?

We want the Australian government to begin negotiations with China to establish a pan-Asian university—a premier institute for Asia—as has been suggested by Professor Ross Garnaut. Through a formal partnership between leading Australian and Chinese universities, students would have the opportunity to study at campuses in both countries. Emphasis would be placed on Asian studies, business and languages. Bilingual and multilingual students could seamlessly transition between languages, reflecting the realities of doing business in Asia. Imagine students building lifelong relationships by living in the same dorm rooms, playing on the same sporting teams and working together as their world views take shape. These are the type of relationships that will entrench our prosperity in the Asian century.

We proposed earlier in this book a significant increase, over time, in the number of highly skilled Asian migrants coming to Australia. As well as helping us to manage our ageing population, new migrants will build a stronger and more multicultural business community, and create invaluable links with Asian nations for expanding Australian exports. Exporters tell us that building their businesses in Asia comes down to person-to-person, trusting relationships with Asian importers. Increased skilled migration from the nations with which we think our economic future lies is a critical piece of the puzzle.

Building links isn't complicated. But it requires funding, co-ordination, commitment—and time. This, of all the changes listed above, is the key to government playing its role in helping Australian businesses into thriving export relationships with our fast-growing neighbours.

○

Beyond our location, Australia relies on the land for our prosperity in many other ways. Some environmental experts say that the contribution of the natural environment to Australia's economy is in relative terms the highest of any country in the world.

Tourism contributes 6 per cent of our economy, and our top spots, according to recent survey data, are our natural attractions. Visitors travel to far-flung parts of our great country to visit natural wonders: Kakadu, the Daintree, the Great Barrier Reef, the Great Ocean Road and Cradle Mountain. Agriculture makes up a smaller but significant share, and would not be possible without nature's endowments—nutrient-rich soil, reliable sources of fresh water, and raw materials such as timber and cotton.

Our environment protects our quality of life in ways we are not even aware of (unless you have visited Beijing recently). Air pollution is estimated to cost the Chinese economy one hundred billion dollars a year due to illness, premature death and lost productivity. Clean air in Australia contributes to a healthy and productive population. Forests play an important role in carbon storage, maintaining soil and water quality, and providing resistance to flood.

Economic growth only matters because it will allow more generations of Australians to live prosperous lives. But not all growth will have this effect. Consider these possibilities: oil and gas mining that threatens life in a marine park; a housing bubble that yields great wealth for financiers but ultimately pops, hurting the most vulnerable and leaving the government to pick up the pieces; growth that drives massive inequality, which undermines the ability of low-income young people to make their own contribution; brief and explosive commodities booms that lead to high inflation and poor opportunities for other exporters.

The old adage 'what gets measured gets done' is as true in government as in business and education. Governments in Australia are focused on GDP as a measure of success. If the economy is growing, good; if not, bad. But growth is not as simple as this. It is not a proxy for all that we value. What are the drivers of our growth and how sustainable are they? How are we using the benefits of growth to invest in future generations? What does growth do to our health, environment and well-being?

Each quarter Australia releases its national accounts—quarterly statistics on how much the economy has grown, as well as ancillary measures such as building approvals and business confidence. We also receive no shortage of updates about the state of government finances.

Yet these measures do not provide metrics on the questions posed above about the environment, equality, social outcomes and the likely health of future generations.

Like quarterly growth results for CEOs, narrowly focused metrics encourage decision-makers (and the journalists who keep them accountable) to focus too much on Australia's short-term growth trajectory. We want the budget and Australia's national accounts to include analyses of inequality in Australia and how it is changing. Clear metrics should measure the impact of the budget and government regulation on our environment, as well as broader measures of health and well-being. Spending on long-term investments (infrastructure, education, preventative health) should be separated from recurrent expenditure (everyday spending on welfare, hospitals, road maintenance) in the federal budget, so that the nation can clearly identify how governments are balancing the needs of Australia today and in the future.

Protecting our environment is part of, not anathema to, long-term growth. If we allow the environment to degrade beyond a certain point—animals to become extinct, rainforests to be logged, air quality to deteriorate—our economy will suffer, and so will our quality of life. Yet Australians today have little objective information about how our environment is changing over time, and the trade-offs that are being made. We support the introduction of a national environment account that outlines, from year to year, the change in the value of our environmental assets state by state over the previous quarter.

A recent paper in *Ecological Economics* contrasts a genuine progress indicator (GPI) with the commonly used measure of GDP. The GPI adjusts traditional economic indicators using factors that diminish and enhance welfare. Negative adjustments include environmental damage, underemployment, crime, loss of leisure time and income inequality. GPI rises with higher levels of education, child care and volunteer work. For the seventeen countries in the study the authors find that, unlike GDP, GPI has not increased since 1978. The GPI is not perfect, but our starting point when developing measures that reflect the health of our society ought to be our values. We value a lot more than quarterly GDP figures can tell us.

○

Australia's current prosperity is the result of a cocktail of ingredients, some hard won, others naturally endowed. Our proximity to the fastest-growing economies in the world, massive resource wealth, strong institutions, sound economic policy and a highly educated population have all played their part in wealth creation. The years ahead, though, look different.

There is probably no other country as well positioned for future growth as Australia. But we will not get there by coasting. In 2040, will Australia be a high-skill, high-wage economy in which our best assets are our educated, entrepreneurial people? Will our businesses have formed thriving relationships with Asian customers? And will our economy be growing—but in a fair and sustainable manner? It will come down to policy choices, good government and a willingness to tackle the challenges we face.

	Drivers of recent prosperity	Challenges through to 2040	A plan for growth
Policy	Strong economic institutions	Institutions remain strong, but vigilance is essential	Review financial system each decade and after significant economic events Continue bipartisan focus
	Good policy	Economic reform harder to undertake and delivering fewer benefits; traditional economic reform may be a less-important driver of growth	Nail the no-brainers: broadband, pricing pollution, raising superannuation rate Continue incrementally improving competition policy Transform innovation policy to help shape a more diverse, specialised, entrepreneurial, digital economy
People	Favourable demographics	Ageing population	Increase rate of skilled migration Improve participation of Australian women: fix child care, address discrimination
	Educated population	Without policy change, will no longer drive growth: education system in comparative decline	Commit to being a top-three education system by 2040 Transform teacher education, pay and prestige Turn around performance in low-ranked schools
Place	Lots of arable land; beautiful natural environment	Opportunity remains, but changing climate and other environmental degradation threaten long-term viability	Create environmental accounts to show trade-offs between environment and growth Broaden national accounts to holistic measures of progress
	Resource wealth	Will continue to drive growth, but only with good policy	Review management of recent resources boom through Productivity Commission inquiry Get policy settings right before next boom is upon us Consider models to ensure future booms aren't wasted: independent advice on whether increased revenues are one-off or permanent; separate investment and recurrent expenditures in federal budget
	Proximity to and trading relationships with Asia	A huge opportunity, but not a fait accompli	Build person-to-person links with Asia Make Asian languages compulsory in primary school; reduce funding for other languages Engage Australia's Asian diaspora Improve rigour and transparency of free-trade negotiations

6

The World

AUSTRALIA MIGHT NOT share any land borders with other countries, but it's not an island. We're twenty-four million people whose prosperity and security are heavily shaped by what the more than seven billion people beyond our coastline are doing. Building on the foundations of the world's oldest continuous culture, the contributions of people from around the globe have created one of the world's most prosperous societies. Throughout our history, we've relied on foreign investment to fund development, to build cities, and to bankroll public and private infrastructure. We've ridden on the sheep's back and in the mining truck's cab to economic prosperity, through international trade. We've welcomed millions of migrants in gold rushes, and in assisted-migration and skilled-migrant programs. Australia is the nation that it is today because of the investment, trade and people that have come here from overseas.

The world has been particularly kind to Australia in recent times.

Regional stability, accompanied by booming economic growth, allowed Australia to open its economy to the world—to reap the dividends of international trade and investment without being confronted by difficult strategic questions.

But Australia is about to be taken out of its international comfort zone. Over the next twenty years we will face the biggest changes to our strategic environment since the arrival of the First Fleet. The foundation of our strategic and defence policy for generations, the United States' unchallenged supremacy in our region, is ebbing away. In its place a new order is emerging, in which more nations will exercise power in our region and non-state actors will exert more influence on the international environment than ever before.

Responding to these new realities will demand more of the Australian community and our leaders, and more of our foreign and defence policies. Yet the implications of this epochal change are rarely remarked upon, let alone debated, in mainstream Australian politics. Political strategists and media commentators alike agree that in Australia there are no votes to be won by talking about foreign and security policy. The MPs lining up for press conferences at the doors of Parliament House know that it's considered politically soft-headed and, worse, self-indulgent to engage with 'the vision thing' on Australia's role in the world. Unless they're playing the posturing unilateralist or pushing a barrow for a particular domestic constituency, our leaders generally downplay or apologise for their engagement with international issues. For every Whitlam, Keating or Rudd who attempts to champion an activist international agenda for Australia, there's an accompanying barrage of negative press.

As a result, our political debate is preoccupied with our own backyard, fixated on the partisan and the parochial. We need a change in mindset—fast. Unless our domestic politics engages the Australian public with the new realities of our international environment, we risk sleepwalking through the biggest economic and strategic change in human history: the rise of the Indo-Pacific.

○

The economic growth sweeping through Northeast Asia, Southeast Asia and the subcontinent is reshaping the strategic environment of the Indo-Pacific and the globe. It's likely that this growth will continue for some decades yet, overturning many of the fundamental assumptions behind the existing regional strategic order. Hugh White, Professor of Strategic Studies at the Australian National University, describes the shift confronting our nation most starkly: 'Only twenty years ago Australia's economy was as big as China's, bigger than India's, and bigger than the whole of the Association of Southeast Asian Nations put together.' Now, on mid-range projections, in two decades China will have overtaken the United States as the richest country in the world; and, as already mentioned, two-thirds of every dollar of wealth created globally by 2040 will come from our region.

As the economies of the major Indo-Pacific countries expand, the stage of international politics gets more crowded. While China will become the most powerful nation in the region by some margin, others too are growing. Over the next two decades India will become more populous than China and could realise enormous economic progress of its own. According to some forecasts, Indonesia could become one of the six largest economies in the world by GDP, possibly even the fourth-largest in terms of purchasing power parity. South Korea is likely to continue to grow strongly, and Japan will remain one of the largest economies in the world. The United States, too, will remain in the top tier of economies in the foreseeable future and is unlikely to withdraw its substantial military presence in the Indo-Pacific.

The next two decades will be characterised by a multipolar security order in the Indo-Pacific, in which China and the United States will dominate but a number of other nations will have sufficient power to constrain the actions of the two great powers. During the next twenty years, strategic power in our region will be exercised not just in Beijing and Washington, but also in New Delhi, Jakarta, Hanoi, Seoul, Tokyo and, potentially, Canberra.

This evolving order has triggered growing security tensions, as countries seek to shore up their strategic position. China's economic growth has been accompanied by even more rapid expansion in the size of its military—it is the second-largest defence spender in the world by some margin. Other nations in the Indo-Pacific have increased their defence spending in response; collectively, Asia has outspent Europe on defence in each year since 2012.

This region-wide military build-up has already dramatically changed the strategic maritime environment in the region. The sea lanes of the Indo-Pacific are now the pulsing arteries of the international economy. More than two-thirds of the world's trade moves on ships passing through the crowded sea lanes that run down the east coast of the Asian continent, above the northwest of Australia and on to the Persian Gulf. Australia has a major strategic interest in these sea lanes: trade makes up more than one-third of our economy, and trade with Asia alone, much of it travelling through these sea lanes, makes up around one-quarter of our GDP.

In recent decades the United States has exercised 'sea control' in the Indo-Pacific: the ability to move its military forces anywhere on water while protecting them from the air and naval forces of other nations. However, denying another nation sea control is much easier than maintaining it yourself; it's harder to control an entire region than to prevent someone else from doing so. In the coming decades, rather than one power having the ability to exercise sea control in the region, it's likely that half a dozen countries will be able to exercise 'sea denial'. This doesn't mean that these areas will cease to be free to commercial shipping or that the sea lanes will be in danger; just that the areas will become more strategically contested and, from a security perspective, more complex to manage.

We're already seeing more frequent conflicts and stand-offs between maritime vessels as nations pursue their economic and strategic interests. The decades-long maritime dispute over the South China Sea, a site of armed conflict in the 1970s as well as of some of the busiest sea lanes in the world, has become particularly volatile and contested. The East China Sea has seen similarly tense disputes, including the establishment of a Chinese Air Defence Identification Zone in 2014. Additionally, longstanding tensions simmer across the Taiwan Strait, on the Korean Peninsula, and in land-based territorial disputes between China, India and Pakistan. Any of these friction points could escalate into a serious regional conflict. That these disputes have not been able to be resolved through either established international institutions or through newer regional structures is not encouraging for the long-term stability of our region or its existing institutional framework.

Looming over these territorial tensions is the relationship between China and the United States. While China has been careful to emphasise its intentions for a 'peaceful rise', it is nevertheless seeking to change the international status quo and gain influence in the regional order commensurate with its position. China is already economically larger, relative to the United States, than the Soviet Union was at any point in the Cold War. While China lags behind the United States in relative military size, in the long run military might is determined by economic strength. In this regard, China is better placed than the Soviet Union ever was to exercise geopolitical power over a sustained period.

The key question for everyone with an interest in the region is whether the geopolitical rebalancing caused by the economic rise and military build-up of the Indo-Pacific is likely to result in a conflict involving these nations. Some analysts argue that history shows the region will not be able to adapt to the rise of China as a great power without triggering a conflict involving the existing great power, the United States. Others argue that this time is different and the costs of a conflict would be too high, because of the unprecedented economic integration of the region. We can make a few predictions about the possible scenarios between these two extremes.

China won't, and shouldn't have to, accept international respect and influence beneath its status as an emerging great power. With China's growing nationalist sentiments and internal political pressures, it's possible that the country's leaders would not be able to accept anything less, even if they wanted to. On the other hand, it's unlikely that China's new status would passively be accommodated by other powers in the region, given the long history of antagonism and suspicion between them. China could seek to exercise influence in the region through coercive force. But it has vigorously rejected such an approach so far, and we think the use of force is probably unlikely because of the economic costs to China's own development. Still, it would be foolish to dismiss the idea outright.

Hugh White argues that the only broadly beneficial new

international power structure that would be feasible for the countries of the region to pursue is an arrangement in which the larger nations share power as equals, with major decisions negotiated between parties and deference shown to differing national interests. He acknowledges that a 'Concert of Asia' would be difficult to manage, but it would also be the only realistic way of avoiding a period of intense, unconstrained competition between China and the United States, leading to an inevitable confrontation.

Yet we don't think that White's Concert of Asia offers a durable means of avoiding such an outcome. It's questionable whether the concessions on sovereignty required to make such an arrangement work would be acceptable to the majority of voters in the democratic nations of the region. Even if all nations with an interest in the matter could be convinced that it was the best course, maintaining the balance of power would require a diplomatic deftness that hasn't been observable in the region in recent times.

Further, while the nineteenth-century Concert of Europe upon which White bases his proposal was sustained for a century, those were simpler times. Castlereagh, Metternich and Talleyrand, all brilliant statesmen, did not have to contend with large groups of empowered and highly connected domestic citizens second-guessing their decisions on the internet. Nor did they have to deal with the independent actions of hundreds of ships and planes in crowded seas and skies. A concert arrangement in the strategically complex twenty-first century would be precarious at best.

If neither accommodation nor coercion, competition nor concert, are in Australia's national interests or likely to be sustainable, what is the optimal regional power structure that we could wish for? It sounds prosaic, but the best relationship between China and the

United States seems to be to continue improvising diplomatically with a more structured version of the way these nations engage today. Kevin Rudd has argued for a kind of bounded co-operation between the United States and China in the Indo-Pacific, where shared interests could be defined and trust could be built through working together on matters of joint concern. Over time, the hope would be that any fundamental conflicts between the core strategic objectives of these nations could then be moderated within such a framework of trust and engagement on issues of shared concern. Given the scale of the change in the power dynamics of the region, this would not be easy and would demand much of the countries' leaders, but it appears to hold the greatest chance for avoiding spiralling strategic competition in the region to dangerous levels.

Whether China and the United States work as partners in the region or end up in a cycle of escalating strategic competition will be pivotal to Australia's future. A period of unchecked competition between China and the United States in the Indo-Pacific would hurt Australia by increasing tensions in the sea lanes that we not only rely on so heavily economically, but also constitute the strategically important maritime approaches to our nation. Such a situation would force Australia to take steps to mitigate the potential risks. In this way, even the threat of conflict in the Indo-Pacific has serious implications for Australia.

After the stabilisation of Indonesia under Suharto in 1967 and, subsequently, the normalisation of relations between China and the United States in 1972, Australia benefited materially from the economic growth that was a result of regional stability. It was given the freedom to focus attention and spending in other areas. Australia's spending on defence as a proportion of GDP fell from around 3.2

per cent during the tense decades between 1950 and 1970 to 2.1 per cent during the relatively calm decades between 1970 and 1990, and down to 1.8 per cent in the peaceful and prosperous decades between 1990 and 2010. China and the United States are already competing strategically; it's in our national interest to do what we can to avoid this competition intensifying over the coming decades.

○

International power is not only becoming more multipolar in our region: it's also becoming more heteropolar. We're not only seeing more sources of power shaping international events: we're also seeing altogether new, non-state sources of influence emerge, including media, religious groups, unions, non-government organisations, extremist networks, diaspora communities and multinational corporations.

Wikileaks' publication of diplomatic cables and Edward Snowden's disclosure of espionage activities have had a dramatic effect on public attitudes, political stability and international relations. Unions and NGOs are using public pressure to reshape labour conditions and pay rates in garment factories across the Indo-Pacific, recently forcing a 28 per cent increase in the Cambodian minimum wage. Non-state extremist networks have used the internet to draw recruits from around the world to conflicts in the Middle East and even to co-ordinate terrorist attacks in foreign countries in real-time. Diaspora communities have facilitated the transfer of billions of dollars in investments between their countries of residence and their countries of origin, turbocharging the opening-up of the Chinese economy in particular. Multinational corporations have used their economic power to get governments to reshape trade agreements across the region, and have even sued governments for adverse policy decisions using investor–state dispute settlement clauses.

And, last, the newly prosperous and assertive Asian middle classes are perhaps the most significant new source of non-state power in the Indo-Pacific. On current trends, the Indo-Pacific will be home to the majority of the world's middle class within the next decade. The Brookings Institution has forecast that the Chinese middle class alone could grow by hundreds of millions in the next fifteen years. The political and cultural clout of these new classes is already shaping as a powerful force in the region in its own right.

These various non-state entities are not substitutes for traditional forms of national power, but they are an ever more important influence and constraint on the exercise of state power in our region. It will be much harder for the Australian government to influence our neighbours' governments if those governments have to fight underlying domestic hostility towards Australia. While nations will remain the dominant vehicles for the expression of state power, interrelating networks of non-state actors are gaining influence both within and between nations.

○

Some Australians assume that there is little the nation could do to shape the international environment in the face of these trends. We disagree. When it has actively engaged with the world, when it has leveraged its national strengths in conjunction with other nations which have similar interests, Australia has shown that it has the ability to mould the international scene to our advantage. We were influential in the founding of the United Nations, and in setting up the rules-based international order that is so important to smaller nations like our own. We played a key role in the establishment of

APEC and the G20: multilateral economic institutions that have made major contributions to economic growth in our region and across the globe. We've helped secure the peace and stability of our neighbours in Cambodia, East Timor, Papua New Guinea and the Solomon Islands. And we've been activists in the signing of a range of major multilateral agreements, like the Chemical Weapons Convention, the Comprehensive Nuclear Test Ban Treaty and the South Pacific Nuclear Free Zone Treaty.

Whether we describe ourselves as a 'middle power', a 'pivotal power' or a 'top-twenty nation' is largely academic. We've shown throughout our history that, when we set our mind to it, we can shape the world.

And that's important, as Australia has a wide range of international interests that we will need to protect as our region changes. As a middle-sized nation, Australia has an interest in living in a region that respects a rules-based international order. In particular, it has an interest in living in a region where international norms governing the use of global commons—the air, sea and space—are clear and respected, and the economic interests of Australian businesses and the safety of our citizens are protected. Similarly, it has an interest in living in a world in which the voices and sovereignty of smaller nations are not subject to arbitrary coercion by larger states.

Second, as a nation with an open economy, Australia has an interest in ensuring that economic growth continues in the Indo-Pacific and that free trade, particularly for primary goods and services, is fostered throughout the region. In the same way, we have an interest in promoting increased economic integration in the Indo-Pacific, and in reducing barriers to international trade and investment.

Third, it's critical to Australia's strategic future that we see a secure and stable region which ensures continued American engagement with the Indo-Pacific, and an appropriate recognition of China within the power structures of the region, but avoids active strategic competition between these great powers. The shared interests and values of Australia and the United States mean that the ANZUS alliance will remain a pillar of our foreign policy for the coming decades. The United States has been proving the declinists wrong for a century, and there's no reason to think that its responsive democracy and open economy won't allow it to continue to do so for another century. Australia's strategic priority must be to help shape a regional environment that allows us to continue to maximise the benefits of the ANZUS relationship in a markedly changed Indo-Pacific.

Australia—an open, diverse nation, rich in the human capital required to harness the power of ideas—is well positioned to pursue these interests on the international stage. Thanks to an internationally recognised policy response to the global financial crisis and two decades of uninterrupted economic growth, we possess the authority of success and the influence that comes with it. We have one of the closest relationships of any nation with the United States, and we've fostered independent relationships with existing and emerging regional powers. We're largely free of the worst historical animosities that impede relationships between regional players. We have highly skilled and respected armed forces, supported by the thirteenth-largest military budget in the world. Australia occupies a strategically important geographic location, on the southern fringe of the Indo-Pacific maritime routes fuelling the rise of the region. We control the third-largest maritime zone and the sixth-largest landmass in the world—a position that could be used to project significant strategic influence in the Indo-Pacific.

Yet the drivers of Australia's international influence will decline in relative terms over the next twenty-five years—unless we invest in them now. The economic growth of other nations in our region means that the size of our economy will shrink, relative to that of our neighbours. Indeed, growth forecasts predict that in two decades we'll be living next door to a regional power for the first time.

While other nations will struggle to match the depth of our relationship with the United States, many of our neighbours will also integrate themselves militarily with that nation as they seek security in the new regional order. Similarly, regional peers' expanding defence expenditure will soon see the relative size of our defence budget fall and our strategic influence in this area wane, too.

Unless Australia chooses to invest in the sources of its international influence, its ability to shape the international environment will decline precipitously, relative to the countries around us, over the coming decades. Given the scale of the changes occurring in our region and their importance to our national interests, we can't afford to let this happen.

Australia must become more engaged in shaping its international environment than it has been in half a century. We need to commit more time to debating the big picture—what Australia ought to be trying to do internationally—and more resources. We must also be more strategic, building expertise and influence in Southeast Asia that we can use to shape the relationship between China and the United States. Finally, we must take a more devolved approach to the pursuit of our national interests in a world where influence is increasingly exercised by non-state actors: creating individual connections between Australia and our region, building the capability of Australian individuals and organisations to engage with our region, and modernising and strengthening the national identity we project to the world.

○

Let's begin by upgrading our diplomatic firepower: the number of men and women in our overseas embassies advocating for Australia's interests. If we're going to play a bigger role in shaping our world, we need to have the staff and skills to carry out the task. Australia's diplomatic corps is small by international standards—by some analyses, the smallest of the G20 nations.

Our diplomats lay the groundwork for major trade and security deals, and represent Australia's interests in overseas forums. In the past, Australia's ability to ensure that our experts were in the room across the range of multilateral forums was a major advantage over our less well-resourced peers in the region. This advantage is rapidly dissipating as the foreign services of our regional neighbours become better resourced. We need more diplomats to take our message to the world.

The expertise within the Department of Foreign Affairs and Trade (DFAT) is also troubling. Currently, fewer than one in ten of its staff members are proficient in an Asian language. It's conceivable that we have a greater proportion of people who are proficient in Asian languages in the broader community than we do in our diplomatic corps. Indeed, anecdotal evidence suggests that there are more graduates fluent in French than in Indonesian starting their careers at DFAT. We need more experts on the countries in our region within DFAT, and closer relationships between the diplomatic corps and academics studying the region.

○

We often undersell the role that Australia's foreign-aid program can play in shaping our international environment in recent times. The fundamental purpose of our international-assistance program is, of course, the reduction of human suffering. We can't ignore Ben Chifley's call to seek the light on the hill 'by working for the betterment of mankind not only here but anywhere we may give a helping hand'. Justice, decency and a fair go should underpin all the actions of Australian governments, and these values don't cease to be relevant at our borders.

But even if foreign aid weren't the right thing to do, it would still be the smart thing to do. Our international-assistance programs are critical to Australia's ability to shape our international environment. The domestic circumstances of our Indo-Pacific neighbours affect directly the effectiveness of our trade, diplomatic and defence policies. Our aid programs can make a substantial difference in ensuring that our region is stable, secure and growing economically.

To take just one example: the characteristics of the Indo-Pacific make it particularly vulnerable to climate change. The locations of large, densely populated cities and the inadequate public infrastructure within them leaves the region exposed to the catastrophic weather events that are likely to become more common as a result of climate change. Given that most of the Indo-Pacific is ocean, even small rises in sea levels would affect the hundreds of millions of people who live in its coastal cities. Droughts and changing weather patterns will have a major impact on water supplies in many of its nations.

Difficulties in reimposing control over disaster-hit megacities, disputes over access to scarce natural resources and conflicts over managing large numbers of displaced people all have the potential to create serious regional instability. Australia's aid program can mitigate these future risks. For some time we have directed a considerable proportion of our aid budget towards assisting countries in our region to better manage natural resources, adapt to climate change, and build resilience against more frequent and forceful natural disasters. Small investments now in the capacity of these nations could pay major dividends for Australia in the form of greater regional stability down the track.

There are other benefits that flow from foreign aid, too. The diplomats running Australia's campaign for a seat on the United Nations Security Council found that there are dividends from being seen by your peers to be a good global citizen. A stable, long-term commitment to international aid strengthens our moral influence with other nations, improving our ability to pursue our national interests in multilateral forums. It also fosters practical connections between our nation and both recipient countries and other donor nations.

The reverse is also true. Given the long lead times of most aid projects and the level of co-ordination between international donors, abrupt cuts to our aid budget not only undermine the effectiveness of long-term interventions: they also hurt our international relationships and our reputation. Given Australia's enduring interest in a rules-based international community and our ongoing reliance on multilateral institutions to pursue our international objectives, the damage from these kinds of decisions is heavy. If we're going to maximise our returns from foreign aid, we need to ensure our international commitment doesn't disappear when times are tough domestically.

○

The Australian Defence Forces' capabilities (what they can do) and posture (where they're located) have evolved within a decades-long strategic context that assumed ongoing American supremacy in our region. Now, the emergence of a multipolar strategic environment in the Indo-Pacific challenges the fundamental assumption that underpinned our defence policy for forty years. While it is likely that the United States will remain deeply engaged in the Indo-Pacific over the coming decades, the context for this engagement will change dramatically. The end of stable and benign American military hegemony in our region will significantly increase the strategic demands on our defence forces. The escalating strategic risks in our region demand a commensurate increase in our defence capabilities: both in raw funding and in our intellectual capacity to debate defence questions as a nation.

There are legitimate arguments about the form that such investments should take, and we discuss these later in the chapter. Given the scale of the public expenditure involved and the lead time required for most defence projects, these are not easy decisions. But the broader necessity—a greater commitment to defence funding to secure our international interests in a region of rapidly evolving strategic change—is compelling.

Australia currently has the thirteenth-largest military spend in the world and the fifth-largest in Asia, but it's a small fish in a big pond. We have a large landmass and even larger strategic interests to defend. Adequately resourced and intelligently deployed defence forces are the price we need to pay for an independent Australian foreign policy over the coming decades: the national asset that underwrites our ability to say no to powerful allies and neighbours when we need to.

o

Whether in diplomacy, foreign aid or defence policy, our resources are limited. As a mid-sized nation, we don't have the means to be everywhere and do everything. To get the maximum bang for our international-policy buck, we need to get more strategic and target our resources where we can get the greatest leverage.

Fans watching the Asian Cup Final in Sydney in January 2015 might not have known it at the time, but they may have been witnessing the football equivalent of Australia's greatest strategic advantage on the international stage. The most valuable player of the tournament and the opening-goal scorer of the final, Massimo Luongo, is the Sydney-born son of parents of Italian and Indonesian heritage, and he was followed throughout the cup by large fan bases in both Australia and Indonesia. He's the sporting embodiment of a Southeast Asian identity and expertise that Australia could harness over the next decades. Professor Tony Milner, Basham Professor of Asian History at the Australian National University, argues that an Australian international strategy that seeks to build expertise and influence in Southeast Asia could form the basis of our future engagement with China, the United States and the broader Indo-Pacific.

As great powers with global interests, the United States and China are unable to focus the attention and resources needed to develop a deep understanding and influence with every nation in the world. The relationship between these great powers receives plenty of thought and care, but their relationships with the new poles of power in the Indo-Pacific receive relatively little attention. Australia could increase its clout with the United States and China as a strategic partner if it could offer value in the form of expertise and influence with the emerging powers of Southeast Asia: Indonesia, Thailand, Malaysia, the Philippines and Vietnam.

While such a strategy would require us to shift more of our international resources—diplomatic, aid and defence—to Southeast Asia and to keep them there for a sustained period, we have a strong platform from which to pursue such a strategy. Australia has many common interests with Southeast Asian nations. Most share Australia's desire for China's economic growth to continue apace, and for the United States to remain strategically engaged in the Indo-Pacific. As a group of smaller and mid-sized nations, our Southeast Asian neighbours also have an interest in the maintenance of a rules-based international order.

We have longstanding national relationships in the region—our largest diplomatic presence is in Indonesia and we have a permanent diplomatic staff engaged with the Association of Southeast Asian Nations (ASEAN), where Australia has been recognised as the first Dialogue Partner. We've shown that we've been able to use these diplomatic relationships productively when we've committed political attention to it, working closely with ASEAN in the development of the Bali Process on people smuggling and in the creation of the ASEAN Regional Forum.

Australia can also draw on extensive personal ties with Southeast Asia. It is home to large Southeast Asian-born communities from the Philippines (around 225,000 people), Vietnam (224,000), Malaysia (153,000), Indonesia (81,000) and Thailand (61,000). And these are just members of the diaspora communities born overseas—there are tens of thousands more who were not born in Southeast Asia but who identify with a Southeast Asian culture. Thousands of leaders in Southeast Asia have studied in Australia's universities and military colleges, and millions of Australians have had first-hand experiences of Southeast Asia, travelling through its countries.

We also have a long history of defence and counter-terrorism co-operation in the region. The Five Power Defence Arrangements between Australia, Malaysia, Singapore, New Zealand and Britain have facilitated more than four decades of joint exercises and training, contributing to regional security. For periods, we've also worked closely with Indonesia on security matters at a bilateral level.

Converting all of this into pre-eminent expertise and influence in Southeast Asia requires action on a number of fronts. We must change the way we talk about our place in the world. We'll also need to change our international mindset, defining ourselves as much as a strategic partner of ASEAN nations as an effective American ally.

We can't expect to dictate terms within the region. We need to engage in less unilateral decision-making, and in more consultation and collaboration with our neighbours as a matter of course. We need to learn how best to influence other nations through the power of our ideas and our ability to build coalitions of interest. In short, we need to model our thinking and behaviour more on Singapore than on the United States.

Changing our mindset requires a better understanding of our region and our place in it. We should invest more in our diplomatic staff in the region as well as academic institutions, particularly for language training. But we'll all have to change our perspective—politicians, media and public. A lack of widespread engagement has left us confused about Australia's place in the world. While sports fans complain about moves to eject the triumphant Socceroos from the Asian Football Confederation, when surveyed not even one-third of us report feeling like Australia is part of Asia. Around three in ten Australians don't feel that Australia is a part of *any* region. We need our leaders to start telling a new national story—one that frames our future as a part of Southeast Asia, not simply a neighbour warily peering over the fence.

o

Committing to an international strategy designed to maximise our expertise and influence in Southeast Asia should also prompt us to ask a different set of strategic-defence questions.

In the past, too often the cart has been put before the horse in Australian defence policy. We've rushed into capability discussions before we've had the broader debate about underlying objectives, arguing about what we want to buy rather than what we want our defence forces to do. Determining these objectives deserves careful thought and broad public discussion. Without it, we risk making our decisions by default, through inertia.

Defence policy sometimes seems to operate outside mainstream Australian politics. While members of the National Security Committee and Shadow National Security Committee understand the strategic environment, relatively few other parliamentarians are as involved. They're unable to debate defence issues in the same way they could other major policy issues, like health, education and economics. Dedicating time to engaging with defence policy hasn't generally been a smart career move. Australian defence ministers have on average survived in the role for less than a term of government over the past thirty years. And it's been more than twenty years since a former defence minister shifted to another major cabinet portfolio: it's a dead end. The result is a dangerous gulf in culture and knowledge.

There is little dialogue about the ideas that will shape our security future within and between our military and our elected representatives. Similarly, there's no culture of public debate about Australian defence strategy as there is in the United States. There are few generals publishing provocative ideas books. No factions of hawks and doves in our parliament argue over the strategic reasons for military engagements. Both sides of politics suffer from a form of geopolitical correctness, in which robust public debate about strategic priorities is tacitly discouraged. We're lucky at least to have organisations like the Lowy Institute, the Australian Strategic Policy Institute, and the Strategic and Defence Studies Centre at the Australian National University bringing some intellectual heft to the subject—but they are islands in a sea of political disengagement.

The disengagement extends to the broader community. In Williamstown, in Tim's electorate, shipbuilders have been working since 2008 on the construction of two landing helicopter docks (LHDs): the largest ships ever commissioned by the Royal Australian Navy. They are 230 metres long and almost ten storeys high, dominating the local skyline; each deck is the size of twenty-four tennis courts. A single LHD will allow the defence forces to make a swift amphibious landing of one thousand soldiers via four smaller landing craft. It can house one hundred trucks beneath its decks and eighteen helicopters above them. It has a hospital that could serve a town the size of Warrnambool and diesel generators that could power a city the size of Darwin. Naturally, the LHDs' construction costs billions of dollars.

If you stopped a local on Nelson Place, pointed to the hull whose presence has been a part of the community for years and asked, 'What's that for?' you'd get a blank look. Our LHDs are extremely expensive national assets, but their strategic significance has hardly been discussed with the public. Should they be used for regional-stabilisation exercises and humanitarian interventions, or should we be spending billions more to launch fighter planes from their decks? Few Australians could join in the discussion. We religiously commemorate what our Anzacs did one hundred years ago; we rarely debate what our diggers should be doing over the next twenty.

Defence policy has been left to ideologues and technocrats, and the broad centre that gives good policy-making ballast is empty. This leaves our defence policy dangerously unmoored. The significant changes occurring in our region merit a better standard of public debate than they have received in the past.

As part of a new conversation about Australian defence policy, we would argue that our primary security objective should be a stable Southeast Asian region, within which the Australian Defence Forces would be able to impose sufficiently high costs on an aggressor so as to dissuade all but a determined great power from threatening our sovereignty.

This would require air and undersea surveillance and defence capabilities to meet threats to our sea and air approaches (that is, our own sea-denial capability), but also amphibious capabilities co-ordinated across the armed forces to conduct regional-stabilisation exercises. In a region dominated by ocean, a Southeast Asian focus would also require a greater emphasis to be placed on maritime capabilities, particularly undersea detection and defence capabilities, than is currently the case. It should tip the balance towards a serious government investment in the national infrastructure required for sustainable, ongoing submarine and naval shipbuilding in Australia. The digger's slouch hat has been the symbol of our defence forces but, as an island nation in a region dominated by ocean, it is our naval culture that should dominate the national imagination in coming decades.

Setting strategic defence priorities according to our own region may also lead us more seriously to investigate the potential for pursuing common security measures with our regional neighbours. Given President Widodo's ambitions for Indonesia to become a 'maritime axis', there are immediate opportunities to expand our naval co-operation: after all, we have shared strategic interests in the security of the Southeast Asian sea lanes.

It is worth considering whether in the long term Australia could facilitate the development of a regional air and maritime surveillance network that is accessible by our defence partners in Southeast Asia. While there are obvious security sensitivities associated with sharing capabilities of this kind, such an explicit long-term objective would be emblematic of the kind of mindset that we'll need to adopt towards our neighbours in the coming decades.

o

We need to do more than just influence the governments of our region. As we've discussed, non-state actors, even individuals, are becoming more influential on the international stage than at any stage in the past hundred years. In an interconnected world, what the American political scientist Joseph Nye termed 'soft power'—the power to persuade, to influence international public opinion without coercion—will play an ever larger role. International surveys frequently give Australia high marks in the soft-power stakes—the 2014–15 *Monocle* Soft Power Survey ranked us seventh in the world.

But it's less clear that we have this clout where it matters most—in our own region, especially Southeast Asia. Indeed, a 2015 report for the Australian Council of Learned Academies, 'Smart Engagement with Asia', recently highlighted a soft-power deficit in the attitudes and understanding of Asians towards Australia. If we're going to commit to an international future in Southeast Asia, we need to start investing in the sources of our soft power in the region: the individual connections between Australians and the peoples of our regional neighbours, and Southeast Asians' broader perceptions of our nation.

This can start with building institutions that will bring young leaders to our country in the first place. International education has long played an important role in developing enduring personal relationships between Australians and its neighbours. The federal government has traditionally supported a range of scholarship programs, like the current Australia Awards, designed to bring bright young international students to our universities. However, as noted by Dean Forbes, a Matthew Flinders Distinguished Professor at Flinders University's School of International Studies, most of these scholarships are framed as foreign-aid programs and changes in domestic priorities have resulted in changes in the scope and names of these awards over time. These changes undermine the prestige and dividends of the programs for both Australia and their recipients over time.

We think there's value in committing to scholarships over the long term in a way deliberately designed to maximise their prestige in Southeast Asia—that is, designed not as a development program, but as a marker of high status in Southeast Asia. Like the Sir John Monash Scholarships, the program should be named in honour of an illustrious Australian, but in this case one who has excelled in the region—the Keating Scholarship appeals to us, but a less politically controversial choice might be 'Weary' Dunlop. Offering a Dunlop

Scholarship to each ASEAN nation annually over many years would not only bring some of the best minds of our region to Australia: it would also create an esteemed pool of alumni with a common bond.

Australia hosts a range of valuable youth summits, such as the Australia India Youth Dialogue and the Australia–China Youth Dialogue. These programs have produced professional, student and social networks that allow more Australians to interact with and understand the cultures they work, study and travel in. We think it's worth investing more heavily in these networks, and hosting an annual Indo-Pacific Youth Dialogue to ensure that the best and brightest of our region's youth are visiting Australia. We can set up alumni associations that connect these individuals with international scholarship students and use online social networks to ensure that these connections continue over time.

We discussed the importance of increasing the study of Asian languages in our schools in the Growth chapter, but connecting within the region is also about appreciating the differences in the way that other countries do business and practise politics, in getting as many students as we can to experience the cities and cultures of our neighbours, not just the bars and beach resorts. We think the New Colombo Plan, which supports students who choose to study in a non-Australian city in our region, is a great start. But the Erasmus program in Europe saw 270,000 students travel to a different city in the European Union in 2012–13 alone. By 2020, more than four million European students will have participated in the program. If we want to integrate with Southeast Asia, we need to pursue a program of a similar scale in Australia, and not just for those studying international relations but for our business and law, science and medicine students.

Australia has a parliamentary exchange program that embeds

politicians with our military, so they can better understand the defence forces. Why not establish a similar program within DFAT to embed MPs in Southeast Asian embassies, to expand their regional experience and expertise? Every personal connection, at every level, will help.

○

Australia also needs to start investing in our ability to project our soft power to the citizens of our regional neighbours. DFAT's public-diplomacy budget in 2014–15 was just $4.7 million—worldwide. We spend far less on public diplomacy—a critical element of soft power—than do our regional partners. The fate of the Australia Network as an outlet for promoting Australian culture on the TV screens of our region is well known. In its place, we need to build a new Australia Network to disseminate our story through the new, twenty-first-century networks of our neighbours.

Digital diplomacy—the pursuit of diplomatic objectives via online and social-media platforms—is a basic function of the diplomatic corps of many of our neighbours. The US State Department now has more than 150 full-time staff working on it. The Indo-Pacific is the most intensely connected region in the world: more than 253 million people in the Asia-Pacific use Facebook every day. India and Indonesia are in the top-five heaviest users of Facebook in the world. The Chinese have their own, extensively used social networks like Weibo.

Digital diplomacy would be a cheap way for Australia to reach vast numbers of people. Yet, in 2014, DFAT's dedicated resourcing for social media comprised just 1.8 full-time equivalent staff. Our embassies operate dozens of social-media accounts, but they are generally one-way broadcasters and are not part of a broader strategy to engage in a dialogue with our region. As Danielle Cave, a PhD candidate at the School of International, Political and Strategic Studies at the Australian National University, has argued, DFAT needs to establish a standalone digital-diplomacy unit, and implement an overarching digital-outreach strategy that would empower its officials to participate in the online conversation and promote a better understanding of Australia. We agree.

o

Using soft power to promote our national interests requires more than connections and communications channels. We also need to shape the context within which these connections are formed, the preconceptions that people in our region have towards Australia. Our sense of national identity is not only the prism through which we see ourselves—it is also the prism through which the rest of the world sees us. Whether something is understood to be representative of popular Australian identity, or an exception to it, matters to the way the rest of the world views us.

This bigger picture of our national identity is to a large degree politically constructed. Edmund Barton might have said that 'we have a continent for a nation and a nation for a continent', but we're not defined by our landmass. We define ourselves through the shared national culture, values and symbols we build together.

How we define our national identity matters within our borders and beyond them. Within Australia, the scope of our national identity—whether all Australians feel like they have a stake in the success of our society—will play a crucial role in preventing international connections that are not in our national interest, including the appeal of transnational terrorist groups. 'Inclusiveness [is] the essential quality of a new Australian security,' as Professor Rory

Medcalf, head of the National Security College at the Australian National University, has said. Combating the threat of transnational terrorism in Australia will depend as much on the work we do here with individuals and communities to promote an inclusive national identity (including counter-radicalisation initiatives) as it will on the work of the defence forces in failing states.

Dramatic changes in the cost of transport and the capabilities of communications technologies are changing the nature of diaspora communities around the world. Unlike the migrants who set out on months-long boat journeys to Australia with little expectation of ever seeing their country of birth again, today's diaspora communities can remain closely connected with the cultures, politics and economies of their origin nations. Geography is ever less a determinant of personal identity.

We shouldn't be threatened by people retaining their ethnic identities in a multicultural society, but we should also understand that the potential influence of origin communities on international diasporas is stronger than ever before. This means that we are going to need to work harder and more strategically at building an inclusive national identity than we have in the past.

An inclusive national identity depends on the way we talk about what it is to be Australian, but also on the actions of government and citizens. Government policies that discriminate against or marginalise individuals or communities within our society are particularly corrosive to a sense of inclusive national identity. In this new heteropolar world, it's more important than ever that every Australian feels a part of our shared national project.

o

It's just as important that we project to our region a more representative conception of who we are as a nation. Australia is quick to arrange a photo with native animals for visiting celebrities, and there's now a six-hundred-page 'koala diplomacy' manual in DFAT, but too often that's where the cultural exploration stops. Our culture and values have changed over the past hundred years, incorporating ethnic, religious and gender diversity. Earlier this year a survey conducted by researchers from the Australian National University found that more than half of the population believes that being born here is not important to 'being truly Australian', and that almost nine in ten of us believe that immigrants 'improve Australian society by bringing new ideas and cultures'. The overseas perception of what it is to be Australian has not caught up with the reality.

Most Australians are now so accustomed to this that we don't even see it, but the international accomplishments of Asian Australians have been particularly significant in recent times. Our Asian Champion Socceroos include players with Indonesian and Japanese heritage. The top-ten-ranked Australian golfer Jason Day is of Filipino heritage, and our top-ranked male tennis player, Nick Kyrgios, has Malaysian (as well as Greek) heritage. Our Eurovision contestant, Guy Sebastian, has Malay-Tamil heritage; Marlisa Punzalan, who at age fifteen last year became the youngest winner of *The X Factor Australia*, has Filipino heritage; and Australians are frequently members of the K-Pop and Canto-Pop groups singing away Sunday mornings on SBS PopAsia. One of our most successful fashion designers, Akira Isogawa, is of Japanese heritage; one of our highest-earning models, Jessica Gomes, has Chinese-Singaporean ancestry. Terence Tao, the 2006 Fields Medal winner (sometimes called the mathematician's Nobel Prize) has Hong Kong Chinese heritage. The internationally recognised political philosopher Tim Soutphommasane has Chinese and Lao heritage. The Silicon Valley CEO (and pride of Footscray) Tan Le has Vietnamese heritage.

The Australian experience is a multicultural success story. Australians from a range of backgrounds are succeeding on the international stage, at the highest levels of their fields. Yet our national symbols have not changed to reflect it.

Among our Southeast Asian neighbours there's little appreciation for the diverse, cosmopolitan nation that we've become. Stereotypes of Australia as a racially and culturally homogenous outpost of the west still abound. Someone in Southeast Asia looking at Australia from the outside might follow Massimo Luongo on Twitter, listen to Jang Han-Byul sing or watch Natalie Tran on YouTube, and even have an Asian Australian friend or relative. But when they see the Union Jack on our flag and the Queen of England as our head of state, they are likely to assume that Asian Australians are exceptions to, rather than representatives of, Australian identity, and that the country is still rooted in the monocultural, colonial mindset of the past.

Dr Timothy Kendall has written an excellent monograph on Australia's relationship with China since federation. He describes how the opening of the first parliament of the Commonwealth of Australia in May 1901 was marked by a visit to Melbourne by the Duke and Duchess of York. To honour the arrival of the royal visitors, locals held a street parade. The traders of Little Bourke Street's Chinatown decorated the Swanston Street intersection with flags, lanterns and a Chinese arch with a banner reading 'Welcome by the Chinese Citizens'.

The dragon-dancers and flag-wavers of the Chinese-Australian community were not citizens. Before federation, the colonies had imposed laws banning the naturalisation of Asians in Australia.

Nine sitting days after the opening of the first federal parliament, the Immigration Restriction Act, better known as the White Australia policy, was introduced. 'Federation,' Kendall writes, 'was a moment of self-determination which presented the new nation with a unique opportunity to reflect upon matters of identity, citizenship and nationhood…[but] the first parliament drew on this opportunity—this moment of sovereignty—to construct deliberately discriminatory and racially exclusive legislation.'

This story has personal significance for Tim. His great-great-great-grandfather John Watts was a member of one of the colonial parliaments that passed racially discriminatory citizenship laws, and his wife is a first-generation Chinese Australian. The conception of Australian identity enshrined at federation, and long after it, actively excluded the family he loves today.

The ethnically and culturally diverse Australia of today is very different from the white Australia of federation. Few Australians would argue that this is not for the better, that Australia in the early twenty-first century is not a greater nation than it was in Edmund Barton's time.

It's time to once again 'reflect upon matters of identity, citizenship and nationhood'. We need to renew our national symbols, to ensure that they include all Australians in the idea of Australia.

It's time to update Australia's anachronistic constitutional arrangements, and become a republic with an Australian head of state and a flag that symbolises the nation we have become, not who we once were. We need to end the farce of asking Australian members of parliament to swear or affirm allegiance to the English monarch and her heirs, instead of Australia and its people, and replace the Queen of England on our currency with an Australian. And, most importantly, we need to forge ahead with the constitutional recognition of Indigenous Australians, to remedy the historical exclusion of Aboriginal and Torres Strait Islander peoples from the laws governing their own land. We need to forge ahead with making reconciliation an ongoing, practical project by replacing the Queen's Birthday holiday with an annual day of reconciliation between Indigenous and non-Indigenous Australians. The treatment of the First Australians is an ongoing sore on the body politic that demeans us in both our own eyes and in the eyes of the world.

We need to do all of this so that our region sees Australia for the nation that we have become, not the country we once were. And, when we speak to the rest of the world, we too will see ourselves for who we really are.

CONCLUSION

Two Futures

WE ENTERED PARLIAMENT in 2013, at a critical moment for Australia. Technology is radically altering our workplaces; inequality is on the rise. Climate change is being felt in a real way; the balance of world power is in flux. Democracy is in decline; we see a rockier path ahead for economic growth. These are the forces that will reshape our nation in the next twenty-five years.

We began this book with a frank admission: we cannot predict the future. This book is not an attempt to do so. But let's say that global trends continued apace, and our governments didn't heed them. Let's say that we drifted into the future, without thought, vision or strategy. What is our worst-case scenario, our picture of life in Australia in 2040 that sits at the edge of reasonable belief?

○

By 2040 Australia's democracy is broken. There is little to bind people in collective political action. The membership of our political parties is tiny, narrow and unrepresentative. A small minority of people support these parties. Perversely, those who continue to engage do so with partisan rancour. The only daily news outlets tailor their output to extreme audiences. Politics is like a soccer match played in front of nearly empty stands, with aggressive hooligans as the only spectators.

In this shallow puddle, minor disturbances cause big splashes. Elected office is a volatile affair, with leaders rising before being quickly dumped in the riptide of a twenty-four-hour media cycle. There are no institutions with the public legitimacy necessary to support a national political debate. No government is able to build a sense of shared national purpose or marshal support for reform. The groundswell of demand for strong leadership is halted by the inability of any party to deliver it in parliament. Long-term structural challenges to the Australian economy have been left unaddressed. When external shocks hit us, Australia's democracy is unable to respond. The lucky country's luck has run out.

○

There are three experiences of life as an Australian, largely determined by where someone is born and what their parents do. In Prosperous Australia, life is easy and failure near impossible. Elite schools and friendship networks provide a 'glass floor' that gives even the ordinary among them access to opportunities unavailable to most. Young people study at prestigious overseas universities, access capital from family funds to start businesses, and graduate into senior management and to board positions of listed companies down the track. Life at the top has never been better.

Life in Middle Australia is different, and there are far fewer people in it. Families work harder to keep up with bills, and few possess enough wealth to feel secure. Conditions at work have deteriorated and a permanent job, with good protections and a good income, is rare. Buying a house within the city or near a train station is a pipe dream, so working parents face lengthy commutes on slow-moving freeways. Australia is more prosperous, but few in the middle see the benefits.

Those in the bottom third live in a Perilous Australia, where life is lived hand to mouth. One slip—ill health, a workplace injury, redundancy, a bad relationship—risks a rapid decline into poverty. For those who can get it, casual work is the norm. Unions are long dead and the minimum wage is a fraction of its former worth. Young people bounce from one subsistence job to another, unable ever to get ahead.

○

The Digital Revolution has changed every aspect of our society by 2040, but Australian businesses, workers and citizens have not enjoyed the transition. Instead of embracing the Digital Revolution, Australia resisted it. When international companies brought disruptive innovations to our shores, we weren't ready for the seismic shifts.

As computerised automation spread from repetitive, routine jobs to more complex tasks like pattern recognition and problem-solving, millions of existing jobs were lost. In their place a new kind of employment has emerged. A job with a sole employer, workplace entitlements and protections is now the exception rather than the rule. The workplace has been atomised by a hyper-division of labour. The majority of workers are now forced to survive on ad-hoc freelance-style jobs.

Our education system failed to prepare our workforce for this new world. A small, savvy proportion of the population earn great rewards from their ability to use digital technologies in innovative ways, but the majority of Australians are left behind. Developers and entrepreneurs look forward to their next product launch, but everyone else worries about the next round of redundancies.

○

Climate change has a noticeable effect on everyday life in Australia, though the changes aren't dramatic—not yet. But when king tides and heavy storms wash away coastline, devastating flooding occurs more frequently and heat records are broken every few summers, you notice the difference.

Parts of the world are on a path to reducing pollution, but toxic politics has kept Australia stationary. The opportunity to be a global centre of clean energy was open to us, but we were too slow to act, and missed our chance. Sun and wind are providing much of our energy, but the economic benefits of the renewables revolution—patents, jobs, investment—have been captured elsewhere.

We have not managed climate-change planning well, and now our only choice is to accept our future: a deteriorating environment, brewing regional conflict and cities that cannot cope with the extreme weather to come. While the real problems with climate still lay ahead, we're worried now, every day, about how the next generation will manage what we've left them with.

○

By 2040 Australians are staring missed opportunity in the face. We're in the throes of the most challenging period of our ageing population. With fewer workers for each dependent Australian, there is entrenched frustration—young people feel they are paying too much tax; older people are disappointed with the standard of their care. Governments are too deep in debt to do anything but tinker at the margins.

We have neglected our young people by failing to invest in them. Our schools rank in the back half of the developed world. Since our education system fell behind, growth in the number of professional jobs has slowed.

Australia is still wealthy enough. GDP growth—powered by demand for unprocessed food and minerals—tracks roughly with population increases. But we missed the big opportunities of a growing Asia. Australians are angry. We thought that a prosperous future was a fait accompli. We coasted, when we needed to act.

○

Rather than benefiting from living next door to the greatest economic expansion in human history, Australia now confronts the risks of living in the most geopolitically unstable region in the world since pre-war Europe. The era of American dominance in the Indo-Pacific is long gone. China has reshaped the regional security arrangements but smaller regional powers chafe in the new dynamic. A web of bilateral security and economic agreements enmeshes the region as nations press for advantage. International institutions and norms have been unable to resolve competing territorial claims, fuelling constant tensions between states. Australia's strength as a resources exporter and, by extension, the strength of our economy, has been undermined by our inability to reach major markets.

During an initial period of active strategic competition between the United States and China, Australia increased its defence spending and military integration with the United States to ensure the continuation of ANZUS. However, an American budget crisis, and the subsequent election of an isolationist president, caused the United States to reduce its maritime presence in the Indo-Pacific, leaving Australia isolated and with a defence orientation ill-designed to protect our interests. We were left feeling vulnerable in the world's roughest neighbourhood.

o

This is one possible future for Australia. But it's not the future we hope for or expect. Looking across the challenges facing Australia in the decades to come, amid the clamour and chaos of our daily work as members of parliament, has taught us a lot about what we can do to avoid the future described above.

While global forces bringing huge change are beyond our control, in most cases we can shape how these forces affect the nation. Australians, by their decisions at the ballot box over the next half-dozen or so elections, will decide how equal our country will be by 2040, how educated our society becomes, whether we benefit from the changing dynamics in our region. And we are optimistic about those choices. There is no country with a better chance to shape its own future. But we need to confront the challenges head on, instead of looking the other way or focusing on short-term distractions until things reach a crisis point.

Evidence will be incredibly important in making these decisions. We cannot make good policy without it. But values also matter enormously. Our national leaders need to explain what's at stake: articulating the principles underpinning their decisions will help the public grapple with inevitable trade-offs.

We need our governments to set priorities and stick to them over time. Australia's political system and media sometimes reward those who focus on the urgent at the expense of the important. But if we allow our policy priorities to be determined by the next media cycle, the next interview, the next speech, we'll all lose sight of the vision for Australia over the long term. We can see the temptations and distractions, even after a short time in the parliament. Many of the problems we discuss in this book require policies and investments that are unlikely to deliver results within an election cycle or even a political career, let alone a media cycle. They can easily be lost amid the small disasters that hit politics almost every day.

Sticking to an agenda is a lot easier with a functional democracy, and that means some semblance of bipartisanship—or at least an end to the negativity that poisons parliament today. There are lots of things in *Two Futures* on which we will never reach consensus with MPs from other parties. But there is common ground. Innovation, early-childhood education, international security and the health of our democratic institutions are all areas where we see potential to work across the aisles. For contested areas of policy, maintaining long-term focus means making cogent, thoughtful, persuasive arguments to the Australian people. In this way, we can make some policies bipartisan by default, where no party can win an election from the other side of the debate.

Politicians and governments will come and go over the next twenty-five years. But institutions will endure and give us the best hope for long-term commitment to policies. Institutions are what keep us honest. They're a respected and well-resourced scientific community. They're independent bodies—like the Reserve Bank, the Parliamentary Budget Office, the Productivity Commission and our public broadcasters—that can call out political opportunists. They're a public service with the expertise and resources to be a powerhouse of policy generation. We have to fight to protect them—these are the tools we'll need to build a future that we're proud of.

So, what's possible if we get it right? What kind of a future can Australia aspire to in 2040 if we learn these lessons?

○

By 2040, Australia is reaping the dividends of two decades of innovation and investment in the institutions of our democracy. Over this period many innovations were tried and discarded, but a long-term focus on improving the responsiveness and legitimacy of our democratic institutions ultimately paid off.

Australians have a direct say in the issues to be debated by political parties and parliament. By allowing online single-issue campaign groups into our democratic institutions, more Australians are now engaged with our democracy. Schools tune in to watch questions posed by students over the internet from their classrooms being answered by the prime minister in question time; community groups propose issues for parliamentary debate, gain support for them in the community and watch them being addressed by MPs.

Momentum for a number of sensitive reform packages has been built through citizen juries. The path to successful reform has also become smoother through the fostering of a more deliberative media environment, anchored by public broadcasters, tax-exempt newspapers focused on serious journalism and a more digitally literate audience.

○

In this Australia there are risks, but we have more safeguards and opportunities. The life-expectancy gap between Indigenous

Australians and non-Indigenous Australians has almost closed. When young people get ahead, they deserve it. A child growing up in Redfern or Elizabeth has nearly the same chance of becoming a cabinet minister as a kid growing up on Sydney's North Shore or the eastern suburbs of Melbourne.

Most Australians can find decent and well-paid work. Early intervention helps children born into those families struggling the most. Australia has the best early-childhood education model in the world; on the first day of school, there is just a small achievement gap between kids from low- and high-income households. By Year 6, the gap is gone.

Reforms to housing-investment concessions and urban planning have enabled Australians across the income spectrum to settle in homes close to their workplace or state-of-the-art public-transport hubs.

The *BRW* Rich 200 List is brimming with people of intelligence, from all races and backgrounds, who have invented and commercialised something valuable. The land of opportunity and its egalitarian spirit are alive and well.

o

Australian businesses, citizens and governments are leaders in the Digital Revolution. Our educated workers are admired internationally and highly sought-after. Children are taught to understand computational thinking, along with reading, writing and arithmetic, and know how to identify and exploit the possibilities of digital disruption. An Australian start-up uses the venture capital it attracted after winning an open-innovation challenge funded by the Department of Transport to commercialise a 'transport cloud' platform of self-driving cars hailed by smartphones. Start-ups and high-end international-services businesses alike relocate to Australia to take advantage of our skilled workforce and environment of creative innovation.

Policy-makers have harnessed online communities to stimulate a productivity boom in public services. Australians in online communities help each other to solve problems and government to improve the way it delivers health, education and human services. Government uses expanded data collection and analysis to develop more responsive and efficient services. A national network of road sensors that can be mixed into bitumen as it's laid produces data that reduces spending on roads by billions and informs new policy initiatives that heighten road safety.

○

Australia has capitalised on its massive endowments in land, sun and wind, and smart, entrepreneurial young scientists from around the world flock to Perth and Brisbane, our renewable-technologies global centres of excellence. Clean-energy jobs are the fastest-growing area of our economy. The explosive progress in this sector has spurred new waves of innovation across science and manufacturing. Community-owned energy is now the norm and electric cars link seamlessly with electricity grids. CSIRO scientists have created a new wave of drought-resistant crops, and Australian farmers are profiting from a booming carbon-offset market.

The short-term costs of adjustment to a low-carbon economy were shared fairly. A strong safety net and large-scale retraining programs for workers have ensured that those with the most to lose have shared in the benefits of acting on climate change. Australians see a clear path to achieving zero emissions, and this is a source of national pride. We are fierce and respected advocates for global action on the environment.

Governments and communities are ready for a changing climate. Cities are built with green belts to absorb heat. Farmers have access to the best information and have developed sophisticated adaptation plans. Local councils along our coastlines are equipped with the skills to guide communities as they make decisions about planning and development. In times of adversity Australians have always pulled together—climate change has proved no exception.

○

A thriving, well-informed debate about economic reform has been underway for decades, and by 2040 policy change is bearing fruit. An overhaul of our innovation policies is paying dividends, with a boom in start-ups. Our education system, led by a dynamic community of world-class teachers, ranks in the top three globally. Young people from across Asia compete to study here.

We are not just doing business with our Asian neighbours; we are fully immersed in the Asian region. Energetic communities of young people work across national borders to build new companies, investing in and learning from Asian markets.

Australia's treasurer has recently headlined a major international conference, outlining our expertise in resources policy. The nation shares a core belief: that our future economic and social welfare depends on protecting our natural environment. Our economy is vibrant, competitive and diverse and, as a result, our standard of living is the envy of the world. We know that it wasn't just down to luck—and this gives us hope for the future.

○

China and the United States have been meeting for yearly leadership summits for decades, and the trust and understanding that has developed has seen progress made on issues of shared interest, such as terrorism, climate change and oceans management. Australia played a key role in facilitating this. We're regarded as a Southeast Asian power, and have used our influence and expertise in the region to bring multipolar support to Chinese and American engagement.

Australia's position in Southeast Asia was instrumental in ensuring continued American engagement in the Indo-Pacific, as well as greater economic and security integration across the region. An Australian-brokered ASEAN Security agreement has resulted in a region-wide maritime security and surveillance network. Australia's Canberra Class LHDs have become integral to humanitarian and stability exercises, and our defence forces are experienced at working closely with the disaster-response authorities of Southeast Asian nations.

A generation of Southeast Asian leaders are coming to power having long-term personal relationships with successful Australians, many of whom speak their languages. These relationships have been forged within the context of a new, inclusive conception of Australian identity. With its own head of state and a flag that symbolises the open and diverse nation it has become, Australia engages with the world as a confident and independent international citizen.

o

That 2040 vision is as optimistic a vision as the other is pessimistic. But Australia should be optimistic, and aim high.

These are our two futures. They are bookends: our most likely future sits somewhere between them, depending on what we, as a nation, choose to do. The choice—we hope you realise—is yours.

Acknowledgments

WHILE OUR NAMES appear on the cover, *Two Futures* would not have been possible without the help, support and intellect of many, many others.

Thanks to our extraordinarily talented and dedicated former members of staff, Clara Jordan-Baird and Matthew Tyler, for their endless hours of voluntary work supporting this project. You rarely meet people as kind, big-hearted and intelligent as these two superstars. Each has headed off to do great things—Clara in the legal world and Matt at Harvard—and we look forward to telling people we knew them before they were famous.

To the team at Text, we're endlessly grateful. David Winter, thanks for your expert editing and advice (and for putting up with us).

To our families: Anne O'Donovan, thank you for your editing, publishing nous, grand-parenting and so much else—we couldn't possibly do it without you; Brian Doyle, for your warmth, encouragement and patience; Patrick O'Neil, the best damn brother a girl could wish for. To the broader Watts family, thank you for creating an environment where children were encouraged to dedicate their lives to causes bigger than themselves, and where ideas and argument were valued.

In writing this book we talked to scores of Australians with world-class minds full of creative ideas, many of which they shared with us to include in the pages of *Two Futures*. We owe a large debt of gratitude to this dynamic group of friends, thinkers, experts, academics, leaders and public figures, who offered help in so many ways: lengthy conversations, problem-solving, ideas, advice, feedback, corrections. Not only have they guided us to ensure *Two Futures* is accurate and interesting (we bear any responsibility otherwise), they have reinforced our optimism that the challenges Australia faces can and will be overcome. Thanks to Ralph Aston, Genevieve Bell, Leon Berkelmans, Paul Binsted, Steve Bracks, Chris Bradley, James Brown, Andrew Carr, Bob Carr, Daniel Carr, Jim Chalmers, Cameron Clyne, David Coats, Pat Conroy, Michael Cooney, Matt Cowgill, Peter Drysdale, Tim Dunlop, John Edwards, Saul Eslake, Tim Fawcett, Matt Fowles, Ross Garnaut, Andrew Giles, Rod Glover, Nick Green, David Griggs, Barb Harman, John Hattie, Mark Howden, Lesley Hughes, Greg Hunt, Peter Kahlil, Nathan Lambert, Andrew Leigh, Darren Lim, Catherine Livingstone, Stephen Loosely, Tim Lyons, Martin McKenzie-Murray, John O'Mahoney, James Pawluk, Kadira Pethiyagoda, Melodie Potts Rosevear, Nick Reece, Nicola Roxon, Ric Simes, Anna Skarbek, Tim Sonneriech, Tim Soutphommasane, Will Steffan, John Thwaites, Laura Tingle, Michael Walsh, Fiona Ward, Tony Warren, Hugh White, Peter Whiteford, Ralph Willis, and many others.

Thank you to our parliamentary colleagues in the Australian Labor Party, the standard bearers for change in our parliament. Thank you to our leader, Bill Shorten, for encouraging us to talk about big ideas from outside the Shadow Cabinet. Thank you to the Shadow Ministers who have indulged us traversing the terrain of their portfolio responsibilities uninvited. Thank you finally to Labor's 'Class of 2013'. Our entry into parliament might have happened in difficult circumstances, but your talent, resolve and camaraderie gives us great hope for the future of our party.

Further Reading

BELOW IS A reading list to accompany each chapter. It's not exhaustive, but it will allow readers to further explore the subjects discussed in *Two Futures*.

CHAPTER 1
Democracy

BOOKS AND JOURNALS

Acemoglu, Daron and Robinson, James A. *Why Nations Fail: The Origins of Power, Prosperity, and Poverty*, Profile Books, 2012.

Bean, C. 'Is There a Crisis of Trust in Australia?' in *Australian Social Attitudes: The First Report*, ed. S Wilson et al, UNSW Press, 2005.

Bryant, Nick. *The Rise and Fall of Australia: How a Great Nation Lost its Way*, Random House, 2014.

Chalmers, Rob. *Inside the Canberra Press Gallery: Life in the Wedding Cake of Old Parliament House*, ANU Press, 2011.

Coggan, Phillip. *The Last Vote: The Threats to Western Democracy*, Allen Lane, 2013.

Costar, Brian and Curtin, Jennifer. *Rebels with a Cause: Independents in Australian Politics,* UNSW Press, 2004.

Cross, William and Gauja, Anika. 'Evolving Membership Strategies in Australian Political Parties', *Australian Journal of Political Science* 49(4), 2014.

Curtin, Jennifer. 'Independents in Federal Parliament: A New Challenge or a Passing Phase?', *Papers on Parliament* 44, 2006.

Davidson, Stewart and Elstub, Stephen. 'Deliberative and Participatory Democracy in the UK', *British Journal of Politics and International Relations* 16(3), 2014.

Dunlop, Tim. *The New Front Page: New Media and the Rise of the Audience*, Scribe Publications, 2013.

Evans, Harry. 'Parliament' in *Dear Mr Rudd: Ideas for a Better Australia*, ed. Robert Manne, Black Inc, 2008.

Evans, Harry. 'The Traditional, the Quaint and the Useful: Pitfalls of Reforming Parliamentary Procedures', *Papers on Parliament* 52, 2009.

Hayes, Christopher. *Twilight of the Elites: America After Meritocracy,* Broadway Books, 2013.

Hirst, John. 'The Distinctiveness of Australian Democracy', *Papers on Parliament* 42, 2004.

Horne, Donald. *The Lucky Country*, Penguin, 1964.

Latham, Mark. *The Political Bubble: Why Australians Don't Trust Politics*, Pan Macmillan Australia, 2014.

Leigh, Andrew. *Disconnected*, UNSW Press, 2010.

Jericho, Greg. *The Rise of the Fifth Estate: Social Media and Blogging in Australian Politics*, Scribe Publications, 2012.

McLaverty, Peter. 'Is Deliberative Democracy the Answer to Representative Democracy's Problems? A Consideration of the UK Government's Programme of Citizens' Juries', *Representation* 45(4), 2009.

McLean, Ian W. *Why Australia Prospered: The Shifting Sources of Economic Growth*, Princeton University Press, 2012.

Martin, Aaron. 'Political Engagement Among the Young in Australia', *Papers on Parliament* 60, 2014.

Martin, Aaron. 'Political Participation Among the Young in Australia: Testing Dalton's Good Citizen Thesis', *Australian Journal of Political Science* 47(2), 2012.

Martin, Aaron. 'The Party Is Not Over: Explaining Attitudes Toward Political Parties in Australia', *International Journal of Public Opinion Research* 26(1), 2014.

Megalogenis, George. 'Trivial Pursuit: Leadership and the End of the Reform Era', *Quarterly Essay* 40, 2010.

Megalogenis, George. *The Australian Moment: How We Were Made for These Times*, Viking, 2012.

Moon, J. 'Minority Government in the Australian States: From Ersatz Majoritarianism to Minoritarianism', *Australian Journal of Political Science* 30, 1995.

Naím, Moisés. *The End of Power: From Boardrooms to Battlefields and Churches to States, Why Being in Charge Isn't What It Used to Be*, Basic Books, 2013.

North, Douglass C. *Institutions, Institutional Change, and Economic Performance*, Cambridge University Press, 2007.

Norton, Philip. 'Reforming Parliament in the United Kingdom: The Report of the Commission to Strengthen Parliament', *Journal of Legislative Studies* 6(3), 2000.

Pesce, Mark. *Hyperpolitics: Power on a Connected Planet*, self-published, 2011.

Russell, Meg. 'Strengthening the British House of Commons: The Unexpected Reforms of 2010', *Papers on Parliament* 55, 2011.

Sawer, Marian. 'Inventing the Nation Through the Ballot Box', *Papers on Parliament* 37, 2001.

Sharman, Campbell. 'The Representation of Small Parties and Independents' in 'Representation and Institutional Change: Fifty Years of Proportional Representation in the Senate', ed. Marian Sawer and Sarah Miskin, *Papers on Parliament* 34, 1999.

Tanner, Lindsay. *Sideshow: Dumbing Down Democracy*, Scribe Publications, 2011.

Tingle, Laura. 'Great Expectations: Government, Entitlement and an Angry Nation', *Quarterly Essay* 46, 2012.

Whiteley, Paul. 'Government Effectiveness and Political Participation in Britain', *Representation* 45(3), 2009.

Whiteley, Paul. *Political Participation in Britain: The Decline and Revival of Civic Culture*, Palgrave Macmillan, 2011.

OTHER

'Australian Attitudes Towards National Identity: Citizenship, Immigration and Tradition', ANUPoll, ANU College of Arts and Social Sciences Report 18, 2015.

Banks, Gary. 'Successful Reform: Past Lessons, Future Challenges', speech delivered at the Annual Forecasting Conference of the Australian Business Economists, Sydney, 2010.

Bartlett, Jamie et al. 'Social Media is Transforming How to Study Society…', Demos, 2014.

Brown, A. J. 'Australian Constitutional Values Survey 2014', Centre for Governance and Public Policy, Griffith University, 2014.

'Citizens' Agenda: National Survey of Voters: Detailed Results', Centre for Advancing Journalism, University of Melbourne, 2013.

Evans, Harry. 'Parliamentary Reform Agenda', submission to the 2020 Summit, 2008.

Faulkner, John. 'The Price of Political Fear', *Sydney Morning Herald*, 30 April 2012.

Kauffmann, Daniel et al. 'The Worldwide Governance Indicators: Methodology and Analytical Issues', Brookings Institution, 2010.

McAllister, Ian. 'ANU–SRC Poll: Changing Views of Governance: Results from the ANUPoll, 2008 and 2014', ANU Social Research Centre, 2014.

McAllister, Ian and Cameron, Sarah. 'Trends in Australian Political Opinion: Results from the Australian Election Study, 1987–2013', ANU, 2014.

'Making Reform Happen: Lessons from OECD Countries', OECD Publishing, 2010.

Markus, Andrew. 'Mapping Social Cohesion 2013: The Scanlon Foundation Surveys National Report', Scanlon Foundation, 2013.

Nurminen, Laura et al. 'Combining Citizens' Initiatives and Deliberation: The Case of Open Ministry', paper prepared for the ECPR General Conference, Bordeaux, 2013.

Oliver, Alex. 'The Lowy Institute Poll 2013: Australia and the World: Public Opinion and Foreign Policy', Lowy Institute for International Policy, 2013.

'Open Up! Report of the Speaker's Commission on Digital Democracy', Digital Democracy Commission, 2015.

'Roy Morgan Image of Professions Survey 2014', Roy Morgan Research, 2014.

Sen, Hopi. 'Kaleidoscope Politics', Policy Network, 21 March 2015.

Smith, Aaron. 'Civic Engagement in the Digital Age: Online and Offline Political Engagement', Pew Research Center, 2013.

'Tuned In or Turned Off? Public Attitudes to Prime Minister's Questions', Hansard Society, 2014.

CHAPTER 2

Inequality

BOOKS AND JOURNALS

Atkinson, Anthony. *Inequality: What Can Be Done?*, Harvard University Press, 2015.

Brynjolfsson, Erik and McAfee, Andrew. *The Second Machine Age: Work, Progress, and Prosperity in a Time of Brilliant Technologies*, W. W. Norton & Company, 2014.

Cowen, Tyler. *Average Is Over: Powering America Beyond the Age of the Great Stagnation*, Penguin, 2014.

Gilens, Martin and Page, Benjamin I. 'Testing Theories of American Politics: Elites, Interest Groups, and Average Citizens', *Perspective on Politics* 12(3), 2014.

Jaumotte, Florence and Buitron, Carolina Osorio. 'Power from the People', *Finance and Development* 52(1), 2015.

Leigh, Andrew. *Battlers and Billionaires: The Story of Inequality in Australia*, Redback, 2013.

Leigh, Andrew. 'Intergenerational Mobility in Australia', *B. E. Journal of Economic Analysis & Policy* 7(2), 2007.

Kelly, Jane-Frances and Donegan, Paul. *City Limits: Why Australia's Cities Are Broken and How We Can Fix Them*, Melbourne University Publishing, 2015.

Piketty, Thomas. *Capital in the Twenty-First Century*, trans. Arthur Goldhammer, Harvard University Press, 2014.

Rawdanowicz, Lukasz et al. 'The Equity Implications of Fiscal Consolidation', *OECD Economics Department Working Papers* 1013, 2012.

Smyth, Paul and Buchanan, John, eds. *Inclusive Growth in Australia*, Allen & Unwin, 2013.

Standing, Guy. *The Precariat: The New Dangerous Class*, Bloomsbury, 2014.

Wilkins, Roger. 'Evaluating the Evidence on Income Inequality in Australia in the 2000s', *Economic Record* 90(288), 2014.

OTHER

'A Hereditary Meritocracy', *Economist*, 24 January 2015.

'America's New Aristocracy', *Economist*, 24 January 2015.

'Australian Early Development Index 2012 Summary Report', Department of Education and Training, Australian Government, 2013.

Bradley, Denise, et al. 'Review of Australian Higher Education Final Report', DEEWR, 2008.

'Childcare and Early Childhood Learning Inquiry Report', Productivity Commission, 2015.

Cingano, Federico. 'Trends in Income Inequality and its Impact on Economic Growth', *OECD Social, Employment and Migration Working Papers* 163, 2014.

Cowgill, Matt. 'A Shrinking Slice of the Pie', ACTU Working Paper 1, 2013.

Daley, John and McGannon, Cassie. 'Submission to the Productivity Commission Inquiry on Childcare and Early Childhood Learning', Grattan Institute, 2014.

Daley, John and Wood, Danielle. 'The Wealth of Generations', Grattan Institute, 2014.

'Divided We Stand: Why Inequality Keeps Rising', OECD Publishing, 2011.

Douglas, Bob, et al. 'Advance Australia Fair? What to Do About Growing Inequality in Australia', Australia21, 2014.

'Empowered Communities: Empowered People' in 'Empowered Communities Design Report', Wunan Foundation, 2015.

Euler, Dieter. 'Germany's Dual Vocational Training System: A Model for Other Countries?', Bertelsmann Stiftung, 2013.

Frey, Carl Benedict and Osborne, Michael. 'The Future of Employment:

How Susceptible Are Jobs to Computerisation?', Oxford Martin School, 2013.

'Global Wealth Databook 2014', Credit Suisse Research Institute, 2014.

Gonski, David et al. 'Review of Funding for Schooling Final Report', DEEWR, 2011.

Greenville, Jared et al. 'Trends in the Distribution of Income in Australia', Productivity Commission, 2013.

Grudnoff, Matt. 'It's the Revenue Stupid: Ideas for a Brighter Budget', Australia Institute, 2015.

Heckman, James. 'Invest in Early Childhood Development: Reduce Deficits, Strengthen the Economy', Heckman Equation, 2012.

Herault, Nicolas and Azpitarte, Francisco. 'Recent Trends in Income Redistribution in Australia: Can Changes in the Tax-Transfer System Account for the Decline in Redistribution?', Melbourne Institute, 2014.

Hoeller, Peter et al. 'Reducing Income Inequality While Boosting Economic Growth: Can It Be Done?', OECD Publishing, 2012.

Leigh, Andrew. 'An Australian Take on Thomas Piketty's *Capital in the Twenty-First Century*', *Monthly*, June 2014.

Lowe, Philip. 'The Labour Market, Structural Change and Recent Economic Developments', Reserve Bank of Australia, 2012.

McLachlan, Rosalie et al. 'Deep and Persistent Disadvantage in Australia', Productivity Commission, 2013.

Neal, David et al. 'Australian Attitudes Towards Wealth Inequality and the Minimum Wage', ACTU, 2011.

Ostry, Jonathon et al. 'IMF: Redistribution, Inequality, and Growth', IMF, 2014.

'Still the Lucky Country?', Oxfam Australia, 2014.

Parham, Dean. 'Labour's Share of Growth in Income and Prosperity', Productivity Commission, 2013.

Redmond, Gerry et al. 'Intergenerational Mobility: New Evidence from the Longitudinal Surveys of Australian Youth', National Centre for Vocational Educational Research, 2014.

Richardson, David and Denniss, Richard. 'Income and Wealth Inequality in Australia', Australia Institute, 2014.

Shomos, Anthony and Forbes, Matthew. 'Literacy and Numeracy Skills and Labour Market Outcomes in Australia', Productivity Commission, 2014.

'Submission to the Annual Wage Review 2014–15', ACTU, 2014.

'The Distribution of Wealth, Income and Assets', Australia's Future Tax Review, Australian Treasury, 2010.

Whiteford, Peter. 'Australia: Inequality and Prosperity and Their Impact in a Radical Welfare State', Crawford School of Public Policy, ANU, 2013.

CHAPTER 3

Technology

BOOKS AND JOURNALS

Autor, David and Dorn, David. 'The Growth of Low-Skill Service Jobs and the Polarization of the US Labor Market', *American Economic Review* 103(5), 2013.

Benkler, Yochai. 'Coase's Penguin, or, Linux and the Nature of the Firm', *Yale Law Journal* 112, 2002.

Benkler, Yochai. *The Wealth of Networks: How Social Production Transforms Markets and Freedom*, Yale University Press, 2007.

Brynjolfsson Erik and McAfee, Andrew. *The Second Machine Age: Work, Progress, and Prosperity in a Time of Brilliant Technologies*, W. W. Norton & Company, 2014.

Castle, Jennifer et al. 'Nowcasting Is Not Just Contemporaneous Forecasting', *National Institute Economic Review* 210(1), 2009.

Coase, Ronald. 'The Problem of Social Cost', *Journal of Law and Economics* 3, 1960.

Cowen, Tyler. *Average Is Over: Powering America Beyond the Age of the Great Stagnation*, Penguin, 2014.

Gans, Joshua. *Information Wants to Be Shared*, Harvard Business Review Press, 2012.

Goos, Martin and Manning, Alan. 'Lousy and Lovely Jobs: The Rising Polarization of Work in Britain', *Review of Economics and Statistics* 89(1), 2007.

Kennedy, John et al. 'The Continuing Decline of Science and Mathematics Enrolments in Australian High Schools', *Teaching Science* 60(2), 2014.

Lessig, Lawrence. *The Future of Ideas: The Fate of the Commons in a Connected World*, Vintage, 2002.

Raymond, Eric. *The Cathedral and the Bazaar: Musings on Linux and*

Open Source by an Accidental Revolutionary, O'Reilly Media, 2001.
Rosen, Sherwin. 'The Economics of Superstars', *American Economic Review* 71(5), 1981.
Shirky, Clay. *Here Comes Everybody: The Power of Organizing Without Organizations*, Penguin, 2009.
Snyder, Emily et al. 'The Changing Paradigm of Air Pollution Monitoring', *Environmental Science and Technology* 47(20), 2013.
Stewart-Weeks, Martin and Tanner, Lindsay. *Changing Shape: Institutions for a Digital Age*, Longueville Media, 2014.
Sunstein, Cass. *Infotopia: How Many Minds Produce Knowledge*, Oxford University Press, 2008.
Von Hippel, Eric. *Democratizing Innovation*, MIT Press, 2006.
Weber, Max. *Economy and Society*, University of California Press, 1968.
Wing, Jeanette M. 'Computational Thinking', *Communications of the ACM* 49(3), 2006.

OTHER

'AI, Robotics and the Future of Jobs: Digital Life in 2025', Pew Research Center, 2014.
Atkinson, Robert et al, eds. 'Sharing in the Success of the Digital Economy: A Progressive Approach to Radical Innovation', Policy Network, 2015.
'Australian Jobs 2015', Department of Employment, Australian Government, 2015.
Berg, Chris and Allen, Darcy. 'The Sharing Economy: How Over-Regulation Could Destroy an Economic Revolution', Institute of Public Affairs, 2014.
Cassells, Rebecca et al. 'Life Chances for Children in the Lucky Country', Smith Family / NATSEM / AMP, 2011.
'Digital Disruption: Short Fuse, Big Bang?' Deloitte Touche Tohmatsu, 2012.
'Engage: Getting on with Government 2.0', Government 2.0 Taskforce,

Department of Finance, Australian Government, 2009.

Gruen, Nicholas. 'Building the Emergent Public Goods of the Digital Age', interview with ABC Radio National, 21 September 2014.

Gruen, Nicholas. 'Government as Impresario: Emergent Public Goods and Public–Private Partnerships 2.0', Nesta, 2015.

Gruen, Nicholas. 'Plan for Public–Private Partnerships in Cyberspace', *Sydney Morning Herald*, 29 March 2013.

Gruen, Nicholas et al. 'Open for Business: How Open Data Can Help Achieve the G20 Growth Target', Lateral Economics, 2014.

Manning, Alan. 'Robots and Progressive Politics', Policy Network, 14 April 2014.

Manyika, James et al. 'Open Data: Unlocking Innovation and Performance with Liquid Information', McKinsey & Company, 2013.

'Policy Challenges for the Next Fifty Years', OECD Publishing, 2014.

Smith, Ted. 'From Open Data to Community Data: Open Government's YouTube Moment', Data-Smart City Solutions, 27 February 2014.

Simes, Ric. 'Australia's Economy in 2020 and Beyond', speech delivered at the Australian Business Economists Lunchtime Briefing, Sydney, 2014.

'The Collaborative Economy: Unlocking the Power of the Workplace Crowd', Deloitte Access Economics, 2014.

'World Robotics 2014 Industrial Robots', International Federation of Robotics, 2014.

'2015 Occupational Projections: Five Years to 2019', Department of Employment, Australian Government, 2015: http://lmip.gov.au/default.aspx?LMIP/EmploymentProjections

CHAPTER 4
Climate

BOOKS AND JOURNALS

Baer, Hans and Burgmann, Verity. *Climate Politics and the Climate Movement in Australia*, Melbourne University Publishing, 2012.

Christoff, Peter, ed. *Four Degrees of Global Warming: Australia in a Hot World*, Routledge, 2013.

Cleugh, Helen et al, eds. *Climate Change: Science and Solutions for Australia*, CSIRO Publishing, 2011.

Flannery, Tim. *The Weather Makers: The History and Future Impact of Climate Change*, Text Publishing, 2005.

Garnaut, Ross. *The Garnaut Climate Change Review*, Cambridge University Press, 2008.

Gifford, Robert. 'The Dragons of Inaction: Psychological Barriers That Limit Climate Change Mitigation and Adaptation', *American Psychologist* 66(4), 2011.

Gore, Al. *An Inconvenient Truth: The Planetary Emergency of Global Warming and What We Can Do About It*, Rodale Books, 2006.

Grubb, Michael et al. *Planetary Economics*, Routledge, 2014.

Huntjens, Patrick. *Water Management and Water Governance in a Changing Climate: Experiences and Insights on Climate Change Adaptation in Europe, Africa, Asia, and Australia*, Eburon, 2011.

Klein, Naomi. *This Changes Everything: Capitalism vs. the Climate*, Simon & Schuster, 2014.

Kunstler, James H. *The Long Emergency: Surviving the End of Oil, Climate Change, and Other Converging Catastrophes of the Twenty-First Century*, Grove, 2006.

McKibben, Bill. *The End of Nature*, Random House, 2006.

Marx, Sabine et al. 'Communication and Mental Processes: Experiential and Analytic Processing of Uncertain Climate Information',

Global Environmental Change 17, 2007.

Mazzucato, Mariana. *The Entrepreneurial State: Debunking Public vs. Private Sector Myths*, Anthem, 2012.

Moser, Susan. 'Communicating Climate Change: History, Challenges, Process and Future Directions', *Wiley Interdisciplinary Reviews: Climate Change* 1(1), 2010.

Moser, Susan and Dilling, L. 'Communicating Climate Change: Closing the Science–Action Gap' in *The Oxford Handbook of Climate Change and Society*, Oxford University Press, 2011.

Proctor, Robert and Schiebinger, Londa, eds. *Agnotology: The Making and Unmaking of Ignorance*, Stanford University Press, 2008.

Stern, Nicholas. *The Stern Review: The Economics of Climate Change*, Cambridge University Press, 2007.

Stern, Nicholas. *Why Are We Waiting? The Logic, Urgency, and Promise of Tackling Climate Change*, MIT Press, 2015.

Stern, Nicholas and Rydge, James. 'The New Energy-Industrial Revolution and International Agreement on Climate Change', *Economics of Energy and Environmental Policy* 1(1), 2012.

OTHER

'Australia's Low Pollution Future: The Economics of Climate Change Mitigation', Australian Treasury, 2008.

Barnett, Jon et al. 'Barriers to Adaptation to Sea-Level Rise: The Legal, Institutional and Cultural Barriers to Adaptation to Sea-Level Rise in Australia', National Climate Change Adaptation Research Facility, 2013.

'Barriers to Effective Climate Change Adaptation', Productivity Commission, 2012.

Beer, Andrew, et al. 'Australia's Country Towns 2050: What Will a Climate Adapted Settlement Pattern Look Like?', National Climate Change Adaptation Research Facility / University of Adelaide, 2013.

Beinhocker, Eric and Oppenheim, Jeremy. 'Economic Opportunities in a Low-Carbon World, McKinsey & Company, 2009.

'Better Growth, Better Climate: The New Climate Economy Report: Global Report', Global Commission on the Economy and Climate, World Resources Institute and New Climate Economy, 2014.

'Chapter 2: Science and Impacts of Climate Change', Climate Change Authority, 2014.

'Climate Adaptation Conference: Future Challenges 2014', National Climate Change Adaptation Research Facility, 2014: http://www.nccarf.edu.au/conference2014/

ClimateWorks Australia, ANU, CSIRO and CoPS. 'Pathways to Deep Decarbonisation in 2050: How Australia Can Prosper in a Low Carbon World: Technical Report', ClimateWorks Australia, 2014.

Dobes, Leo et al. 'Adaptor of Last Resort? An Economic Perspective on the Government's Role in Adaptation to Climate Change', National Climate Change Adaptation Research Facility / ANU, 2013.

'Fifth Assessment Report of the Intergovernmental Panel on Climate Change', Cambridge University Press, 2013.

Flannery, Tim et al. 'Lagging Behind: Australia and the Global Response to Climate Change', Climate Council, 2014.

'Getting Your Audience's Attention', Center for Research on Environmental Decisions, 2009: http://guide.cred.columbia.edu/guide/sec2.html

Giddens, Anthony. 'The Politics of Climate Change': http://www.dac.dk/en/dac-cities/sustainable-cities/experts/anthony-giddens-the-politics-of-climate-change/

Jackson, Erwin. 'Australians Shifting on Climate Change', Lowy Institute for International Policy, 2014.

Leviston, Zoe et al. 'Australians' Views of Climate Change', CSIRO / Garnaut Review Commissioned Work, 2011.

Mills, Luke. 'Global Trends in Clean Energy Investment', Bloomberg New Energy Finance, 2015.

'Renewable Energy and Jobs: Annual Review 2014', International

Renewable Energy Agency, 2014.
Steffen, Will. 'The Angry Summer', Climate Commission, 2013.
Steffen, Will and Hughes, Leslie. 'The Critical Decade: Climate Change and Health', Climate Commission, 2011.
Steffen, Will et al. 'Counting the Costs: Climate Change and Coastal Flooding', Climate Council, 2014.
Steffen, Will et al. 'Heatwaves: Hotter, Longer, More Often', Climate Council, 2014.
Stern, Nicholas. 'Growth, Climate and Collaboration: Towards Agreement in Paris 2015', Centre for Climate Change Economics and Policy / Grantham Research Institute on Climate Change and the Environment / LSE, 2014.
Stolton, Sue et al. 'Protected Areas, Climate Change and Disaster Mitigation', Equilibrium Research, 2008.
'Survey of Climate Attitudes', CSIRO, 2013: http://www.csiro.au/en/Research/LWF/Areas/Social-economic/Climate-change/Climate-attitudes-survey
'Turn Down the Heat: Confronting the New Climate Normal', World Bank, 2014.
Weber, Elke et al. 'Heuristics and Constructed Beliefs in Climate Change Perception: Effect of Outdoor Temperature, Question Construction, and Cognitive Primes', Center for Research on Environmental Decisions, 2015.

CHAPTER 5
Growth

BOOKS AND JOURNALS

Acemaglou, Daron and Robinson, James A. *Why Nations Fail: The Origins of Power, Prosperity, and Poverty*, Profile Books, 2012.

Brynjolfsson, Erik and McAfee, Andrew. *Race Against the Machine: How the Digital Revolution Is Accelerating Innovation, Driving Productivity, and Irreversibly Transforming Employment and the Economy*, Digital Frontier Press, 2012.

Bryant, Nick. *The Rise and Fall of Australia: How a Great Nation Lost its Way*, Random House, 2014.

Charlton, Andrew. 'Dragon's Tail: The Lucky Country After the China Boom', *Quarterly Essay* 54, 2014.

Charlton, Andrew. *Ozonomics*, Random House, 2007.

Costanza, Robert et al. 'Changes in the Global Value of Ecosystem Services', *Global Environmental Change* 26, 2014.

Cowen, Tyler. *The Great Stagnation: How America Ate All the Low-Hanging Fruit of Modern History, Got Sick, and Will (Eventually) Feel Better*, Penguin, 2011.

Edwards, John. *Beyond the Boom: A Lowy Institute Paper*, Penguin, 2014.

Garnaut, Ross. *Dog Days: Australia After the Boom*, Redback, 2013.

MacIntyre, Stuart. *A Concise History of Australia*, Cambridge University Press, 2009.

McLean, Ian W. *Why Australia Prospered: The Shifting Sources of Economic Growth*, Princeton University Press, 2012.

Megalogenis, George. *The Australian Moment: How We Were Made for These Times*, Penguin, 2012.

Taleb, Nassim. *Antifragile: Things That Gain from Disorder*, Random House, 2014.

OTHER

'Australia in the Asian Century' White Paper, Australia in the Asian Century Task Force, Australian Government, 2012.

'Human Capital and Productivity Literature Review', Australian Workforce and Productivity Agency, 2013.

Baars, Sam et al. 'Lessons from London Schools: Investigating the Success', CfBT Education Trust, 2014.

Baghai, Mehrdad et al. 'Positioning for Prosperity? Catching the Next Wave', Deloitte Touche Tohmatsu, 2014.

Baily, Martin et al. 'Building Long-Term Strategy for Growth through Innovation', Brookings Institution, 2011.

'Building Australia's Comparative Advantages', Business Council of Australia, 2014.

Costanza, Robert et al. 'Beyond GDP: The Need for New Measures of Progress', Pardee Papers 4, Boston University, 2009.

D'Arcy, P. and Gustafsson, L. 'Australia's Productivity Performance and Real Incomes', Reserve Bank of Australia, 2012.

'Developing an Asia Capable Workforce', Asialink, University of Melbourne, 2012.

Downes, Peter et al. 'The Effect of the Mining Boom on the Australian Economy', Reserve Bank of Australia, 2014.

'Economic Impacts of Migration and Population Growth', Productivity Commission, 2006.

Garnaut, Ross. 'Capitalism, Socialism and Democracy in the Twenty First Century', LSE–University of Melbourne Public Lecture delivered at the London School of Economics and Political Science, 2014.

Grudnoff, Matt. 'Tax Cuts That Broke the Budget', Australia Institute, 2013.

Gruen, David. 'Statement to the Senate Standing Committee on Economics Canberra, 22 October 2008', Australian Treasury, 2008.

Gruen, David. 'The Return of Fiscal Policy', Australian Treasury, 2009.

Gruen, David and Wilcox, Rhett. 'After the Resources Investment

Boom: Seamless Transition or Dog Days?', speech to the Australian Conference of Economists, Hobart, 2014.

Hattie, John. 'Teachers Make a Difference: What Is the Research Evidence?', paper presented at the Joint New Zealand Association for Research in Education and Australian Association for Research in Education Conference, Melbourne, 2003.

Henry, Ken. 'Australia's Future Tax System: Report to the Treasurer', Australian Treasury, 2009.

Jensen, Ben. 'Catching Up: Learning from the Best School Systems in East Asia', Grattan Institute, 2012.

Jensen, Ben. 'Turning Around Schools: It Can Be Done', Grattan Institute, 2014.

Lyndon, John et al. 'Compete to Prosper: Improving Australia's Global Competitiveness', McKinsey Australia, 2014.

McDonald, Peter and Temple, Jeromey. 'Immigration, Labour Supply and Per Capita Gross Domestic Product: Australia 2010–2050', ANU / Australian Demographic and Social Research Institute, 2010.

Moss, Ilan. 'Start-Up Nation: An Innovation Story', *OECD Observer* 285, 2011.

Mourshed, Mona et al. 'How the World's Most Improved School Systems Keep Getting Better', McKinsey & Company, 2010.

Murray, David et al. 'Financial System Inquiry: Final Report', Australian Treasury, 2014.

Parkinson, Martin. 'Fiscal Sustainability and Living Standards: The Decade Ahead', speech delivered at the Sydney Institute, 2014.

Pearson, Leonie. 'Sustainable Development: How Can It Be Measured and Modelled in Australia?', CSIRO, 2010.

Phillips, Ben. 'Child Care Affordability in Australia', AMP.NATSEM Income and Wealth Report 35, 2014.

Rayner, Vanessa and Bishop, James. 'Industry Dimensions of the Resource Boom: An Input–Output Analysis', Reserve Bank of Australia, 2013.

Rudd, Kevin. 'The Global Financial Crisis', *Monthly,* February 2009.

Simes, Ric and Gittins, Ross. 'Australia's Economy in 2020 and Beyond: Ric Simes in Conversation with Ross Gittins', Australian Business Economists, 2014.

Sims, Rod. 'Australia's Experience Driving Economic Growth Through Competition Policy Reforms', Australian Competition and Consumer Commission, 2013.

'The High Cost of Low Educational Performance', OECD Publishing, 2010.

'Why Australian Businesses Are Missing the Asian Opportunity: And What They Can Do About It', PricewaterhouseCoopers, 2014.

'2015 Intergenerational Report: Australia in 2055', Australian Treasury, 2015.

CHAPTER 6
The World

BOOKS AND JOURNALS

Brown, James. *ANZAC's Long Shadow: The Cost of Our National Obsession*, Black Inc, 2014.

Charlton, Andrew. 'Dragon's Tail: The Lucky Country After the China Boom', *Quarterly Essay* 54, 2014.

Dean, Peter J. et al. *Australia's Defence: Towards a New Era?* Melbourne University Publishing, 2014.

Frühling, Stephan. *Defence Planning and Uncertainty: Preparing for the Next Asia-Pacific War*, Routledge, 2014.

Goldsmith, Benjamin et al. 'Doing Well by Doing Good: The Impact of Foreign Aid on Foreign Public Opinion', *Quarterly Journal of Political Science* 9(1), 2014.

Kaplan, Robert. *Asia's Cauldron: The South China Sea and the End of a Stable Pacific*, Random House, 2014.

Keating, Paul. *Engagement: Australia Faces the Asia-Pacific*, Pan Macmillan Australia, 2000.

Kilcullen, David. *Out of the Mountains: The Coming Age of the Urban Guerrilla*, Scribe Publications, 2013.

McDonald, Hamish. *Demokrasi: Indonesia in the Twenty-First Century*, Black Inc, 2014.

Milner, Anthony. 'Analysing Asian Regionalism: What is an "Architectural Perspective"?', *Australian Journal of International Affairs* 65(1), 2011.

Soutphommasane, Tim. *Reclaiming Patriotism: Nation-Building for Australian Progressives*, Cambridge University Press, 2010.

Wesley, Michael. *There Goes the Neighbourhood: Australia and the Rise of Asia,* UNSW Press, 2011.

White, Hugh. *The China Choice: Why America Should Share Power*, Black Inc, 2013.

OTHER

Ang, Ien et al. 'Smart Engagement with Asia: Leveraging Language, Research and Culture', Australian Council of Learned Academies, 2015.

'Are We a Top Twenty Nation or a Middle Power?', ASPI Strategic Insights, 2014.

Arup, Tom. 'The Rise and Influence of Koala Diplomacy', *Age*, 27 December 2014.

'Australia in the Asian Century' White Paper, Australia in the Asian Century Task Force, Australian Government, 2012.

Bateman, Sam et al. 'Terms of Engagement: Australia's Regional Defence Diplomacy', ASPI, 2013.

Evans, Gareth. 'Middle Power Diplomacy', speech delivered at the Inaugural Edgardo Boeninger Memorial Lecture, Santiago, 2011.

Fullilove, Michael. 'World Wide Webs: Diasporas and the International System', Lowy Institute for International Policy Paper 22, 2008.

Fullilove, Michael and Bubalo, Anthony. 'Reports from a Turbulent Decade', Lowy Institute for International Policy, 2013.

Gygnell, Alan. 'Parallel Worlds', Lowy Institute for International Policy, 2004.

Hanson, Fergus. 'Revolution @ State: The Spread of E-Diplomacy', Lowy Institute for International Policy, 2012.

Hartcher, Peter. 'The Adolescent Country', Lowy Institute for International Policy, 2014.

'Inquiry into Australia's Overseas Representation', Joint Standing Committee on Foreign Affairs, Defence and Trade, Parliament of Australia, 2012.

Kendall, Timothy. 'Within China's Orbit? China Through the Eyes of the Australian Parliament', Parliamentary Library, Commonwealth of Australia, 2007.

Li, Cheng, ed. 'China's Emerging Middle Class: Beyond Economic Transformation', Brookings Institution, 2010.

McKay, Huw. 'The World Economy in 2100: Five Alternative Visions of the Future and the Development of the Alliance', United States Studies Centre, 2012.

Medcalf, Rory. 'Towards a New Australian Security', speech delivered at the National Security College, ANU, 2015.

Medcalf, Rory and Brown, James. 'Defence Challenges 2035: Securing Australia's Lifelines', Lowy Institute for International Policy, 2014.

Milner, Anthony and Percival Wood, Sally, eds. 'Our Place in the Asian Century: Southeast Asia as "The Third Way"', Asialink, 2012.

Nicholson, Brendan. 'Cabinet Papers 1988–89: A Declining Power: Our Image Problem in Asia', *Australian*, 1 January 2015.

Oliver, Alex. 'Response to Invitation to Comment', DFAT Consular Strategy 2014–2016, Lowy Institute for International Policy, 2014.

Oliver, Alex and Shearer, Andrew. 'Diplomatic Disrepair: Rebuilding Australia's International Policy Infrastructure', Lowy Institute for International Policy, 2011.

Perlo-Freeman, Sam et al. 'Trends in World Military Expenditure 2014', SIPRI Fact Sheet, 2015.

'Public Diplomacy Strategy 2014–2016', Department of Foreign Affairs and Trade, Australian Government: http://dfat.gov.au/people-to-people/public-diplomacy/Pages/public-diplomacy-strategy.aspx

Rudd, Kevin. 'US–China 21: The Future of US–China Relations Under Xi Jinping: Toward a New Framework of Constructive Realism for a Common Purpose', Belfer Center for Science and International Affairs, Harvard Kennedy School of Government, 2015.

Supriyanto, Ristian Atriandi. 'Waves of Opportunity: Enhancing Australia–Indonesia Maritime Security Cooperation', ASPI Strategic Insights, 2014.

'The World in 2050: Will the Shift in Global Economic Power Continue?', PricewaterhouseCoopers, 2015.

Wesley, Michael. 'The 2012 Vernon Parker Oration', speech delivered to the Australian Naval Institute, 2012.

White, Hugh. 'A Focused Force: Australia's Defence Priorities in the Asian Century', Lowy Institute for International Policy Paper 26, 2009.

Yudhoyono, Susilo Bambang. 'Speech by H. E. Dr Susilo Bambang Yudhoyono President Republic of Indonesia Before the Australian Parliament', Canberra, 2010.